THE WORRIER'S GUIDE
★ ★ ★ TO LIFE ★ ★ ★

THE WORRIER'S GUIDE TO LIFE

★ ★ ★ ★ ★ BY GEMMA CORRELL ★ ★ ★ ★ ★

**Andrews McMeel
Publishing**®

Kansas City • Sydney • London

CONTENTS

★ ★ ★ ★ ★

CHAPTER ONE

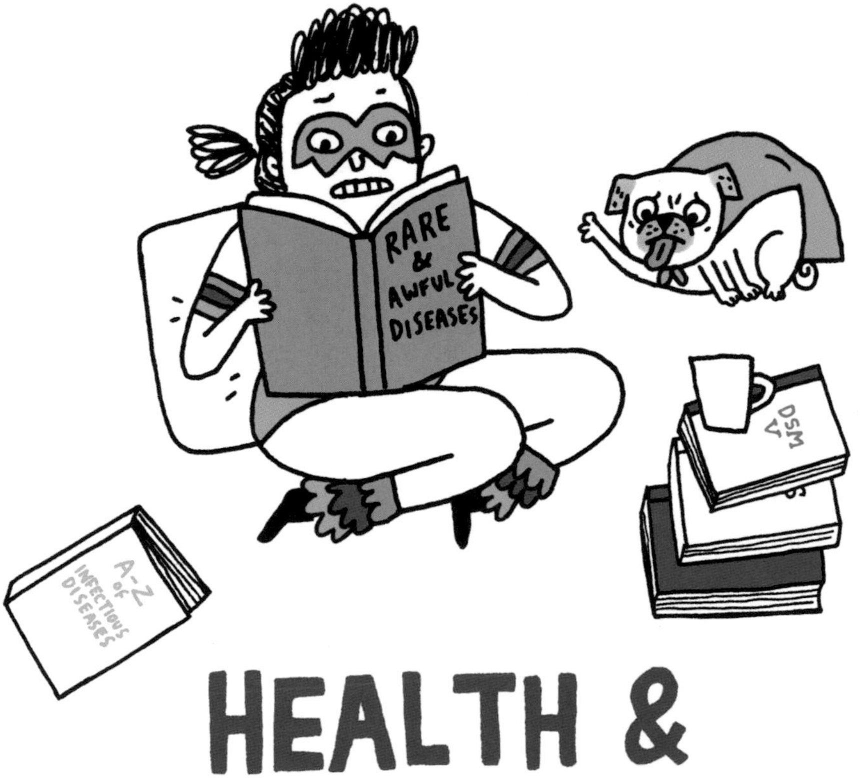
RARE & AWFUL DISEASES
DSM V
A-Z of INFECTIOUS DISEASES

HEALTH & HYPOCHONDRIA

IT BEGINS...

IS MY UMBILICAL CORD NORMAL?
I BET ALL THE OTHER FETUSES ARE WAY FURTHER ALONG IN THEIR DEVELOPMENT...
WHAT IF EVERYONE LAUGHS AT ME WHEN I COME OUT?
WHAT AM I DOING WITH MY LIFE?
I'M SURE I LOOK SO STUPID IN MY ULTRA-SOUND PHOTO.
I DON'T WANT TO GO OUTSIDE.

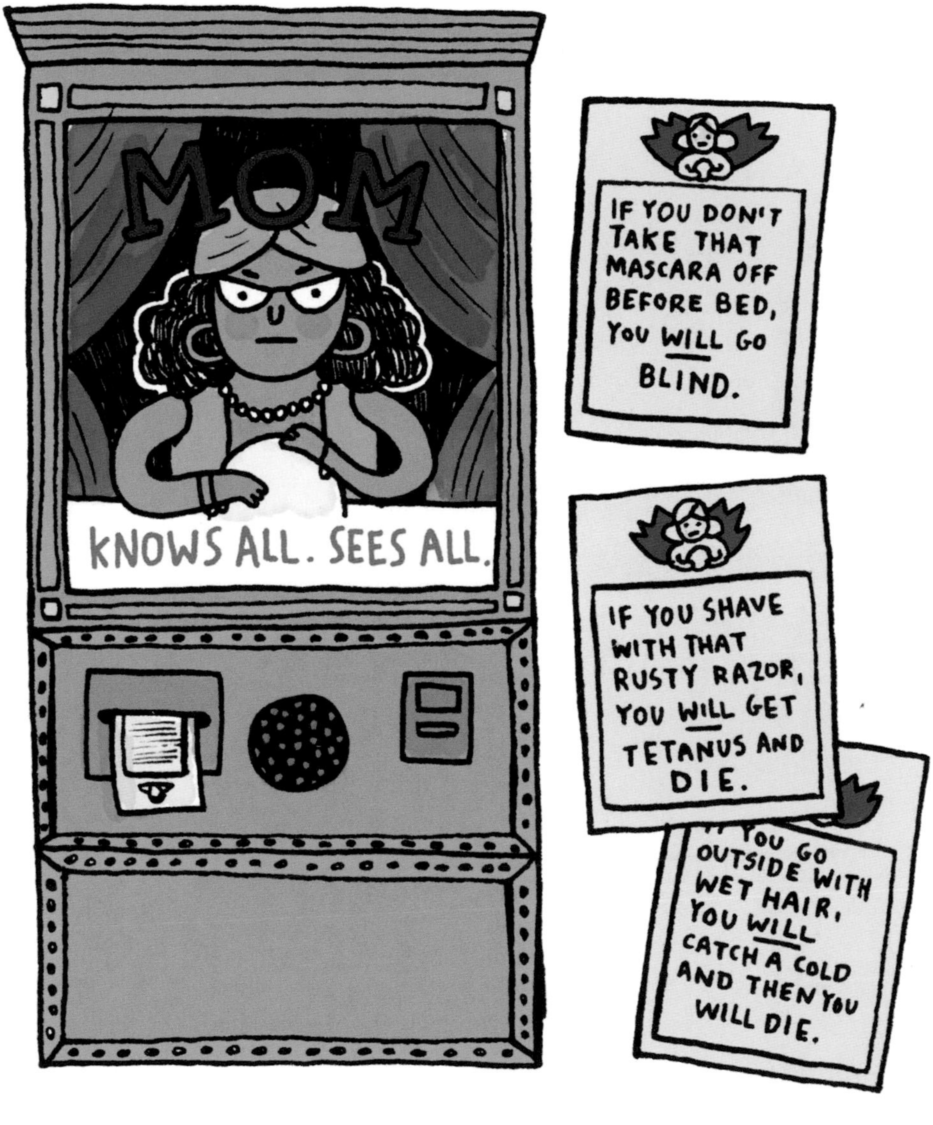
MOM
KNOWS ALL. SEES ALL.
IF YOU DON'T TAKE THAT MASCARA OFF BEFORE BED, YOU WILL GO BLIND.
IF YOU SHAVE WITH THAT RUSTY RAZOR, YOU WILL GET TETANUS AND DIE.
YOU GO OUTSIDE WITH WET HAIR, YOU WILL CATCH A COLD AND THEN YOU WILL DIE.

BODY SHAPES : A HANDY GUIDE

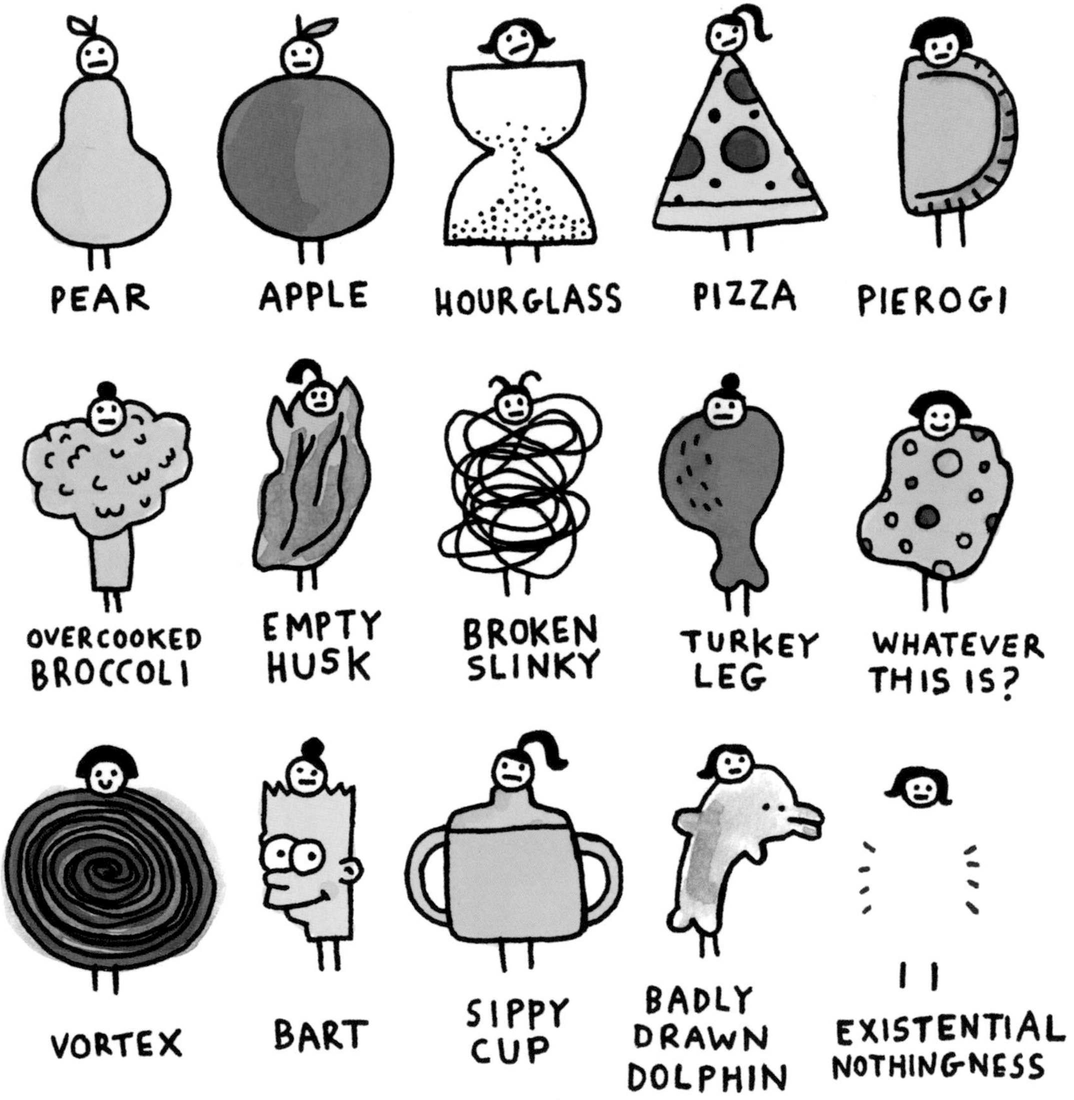
PEAR
APPLE
HOURGLASS
PIZZA
PIEROGI
OVERCOOKED BROCCOLI
EMPTY HUSK
BROKEN SLINKY
TURKEY LEG
WHATEVER THIS IS?
VORTEX
BART
SIPPY CUP
BADLY DRAWN DOLPHIN
EXISTENTIAL NOTHINGNESS

PROBLEM AREAS

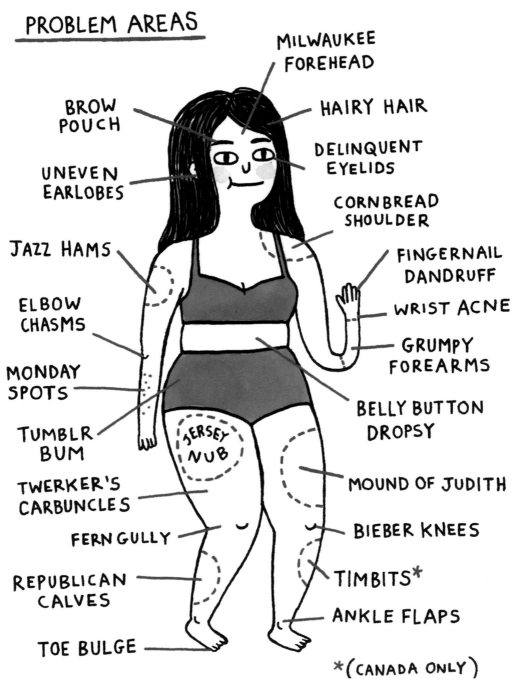

MILWAUKEE FOREHEAD

BROW POUCH

HAIRY HAIR

UNEVEN EARLOBES

DELINQUENT EYELIDS

CORNBREAD SHOULDER

JAZZ HAMS

FINGERNAIL DANDRUFF

ELBOW CHASMS

WRIST ACNE

GRUMPY FOREARMS

MONDAY SPOTS

BELLY BUTTON DROPSY

TUMBLR BUM

JERSEY NUB

TWERKER'S CARBUNCLES

MOUND OF JUDITH

FERN GULLY

BIEBER KNEES

REPUBLICAN CALVES

TIMBITS*

ANKLE FLAPS

TOE BULGE

*(CANADA ONLY)

5

PHASES OF THE MOON

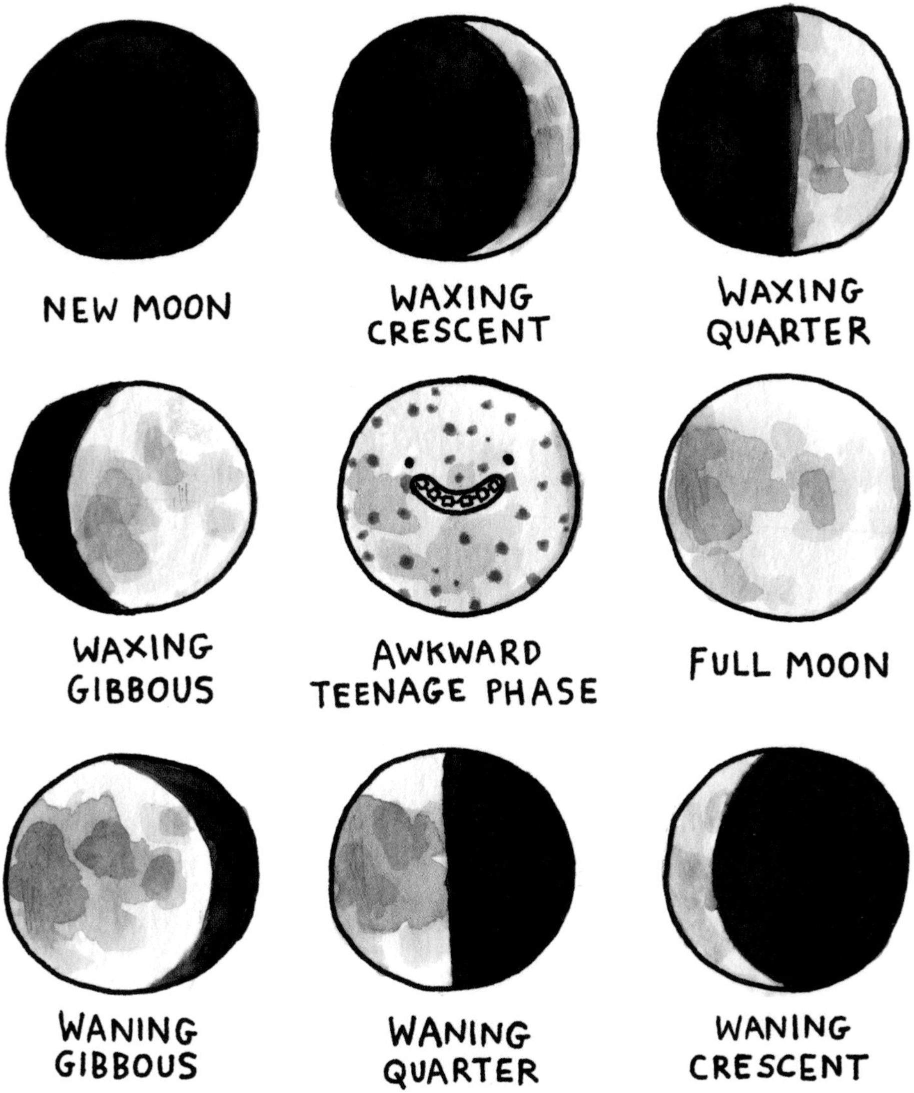
NEW MOON
WAXING CRESCENT
WAXING QUARTER
WAXING GIBBOUS
AWKWARD TEENAGE PHASE
FULL MOON
WANING GIBBOUS
WANING QUARTER
WANING CRESCENT

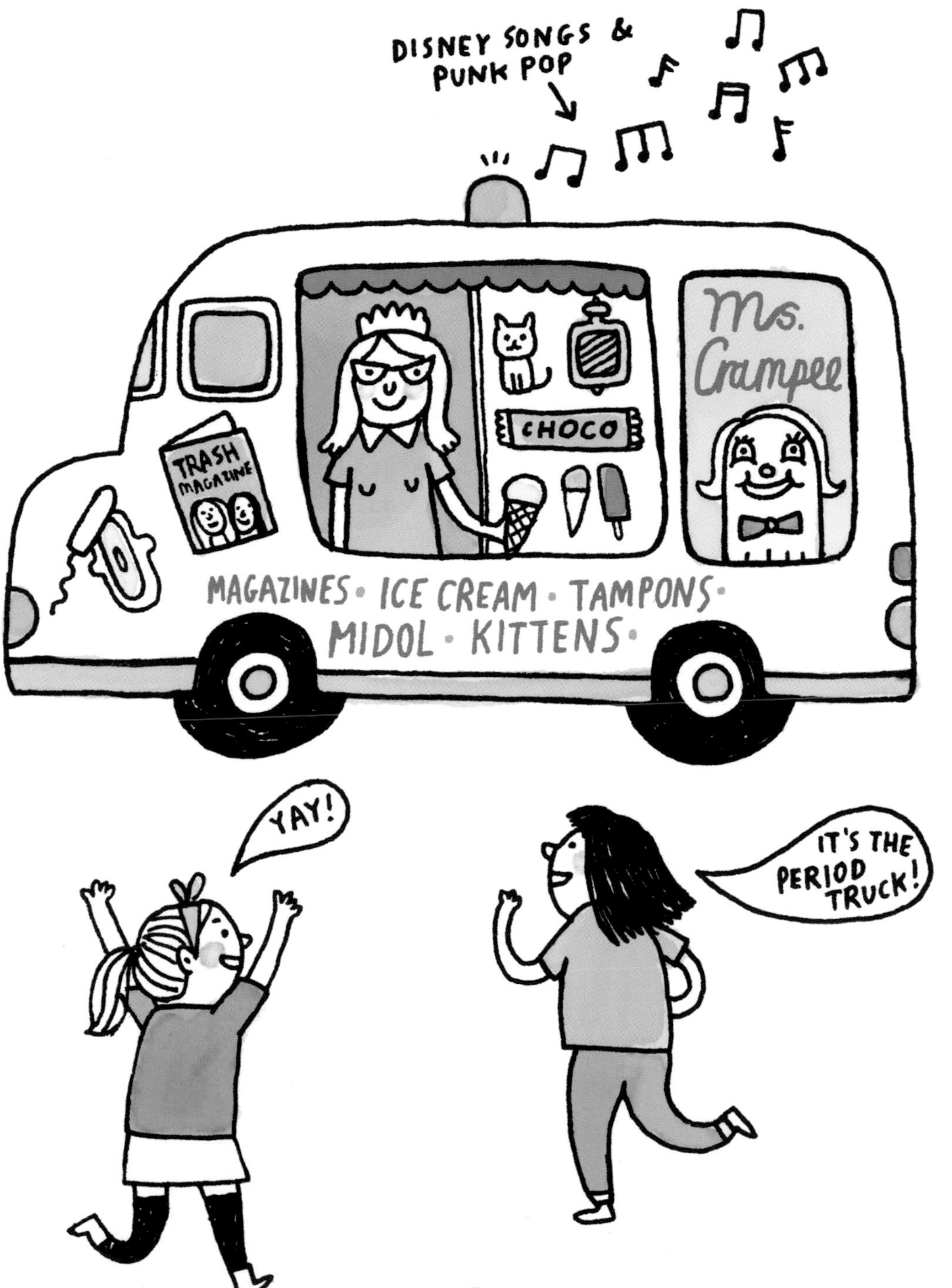
DISNEY SONGS & PUNK POP
Ms. Crampee
TRASH MAGAZINE
CHOCO
MAGAZINES • ICE CREAM • TAMPONS • MIDOL • KITTENS •
YAY!
IT'S THE PERIOD TRUCK!

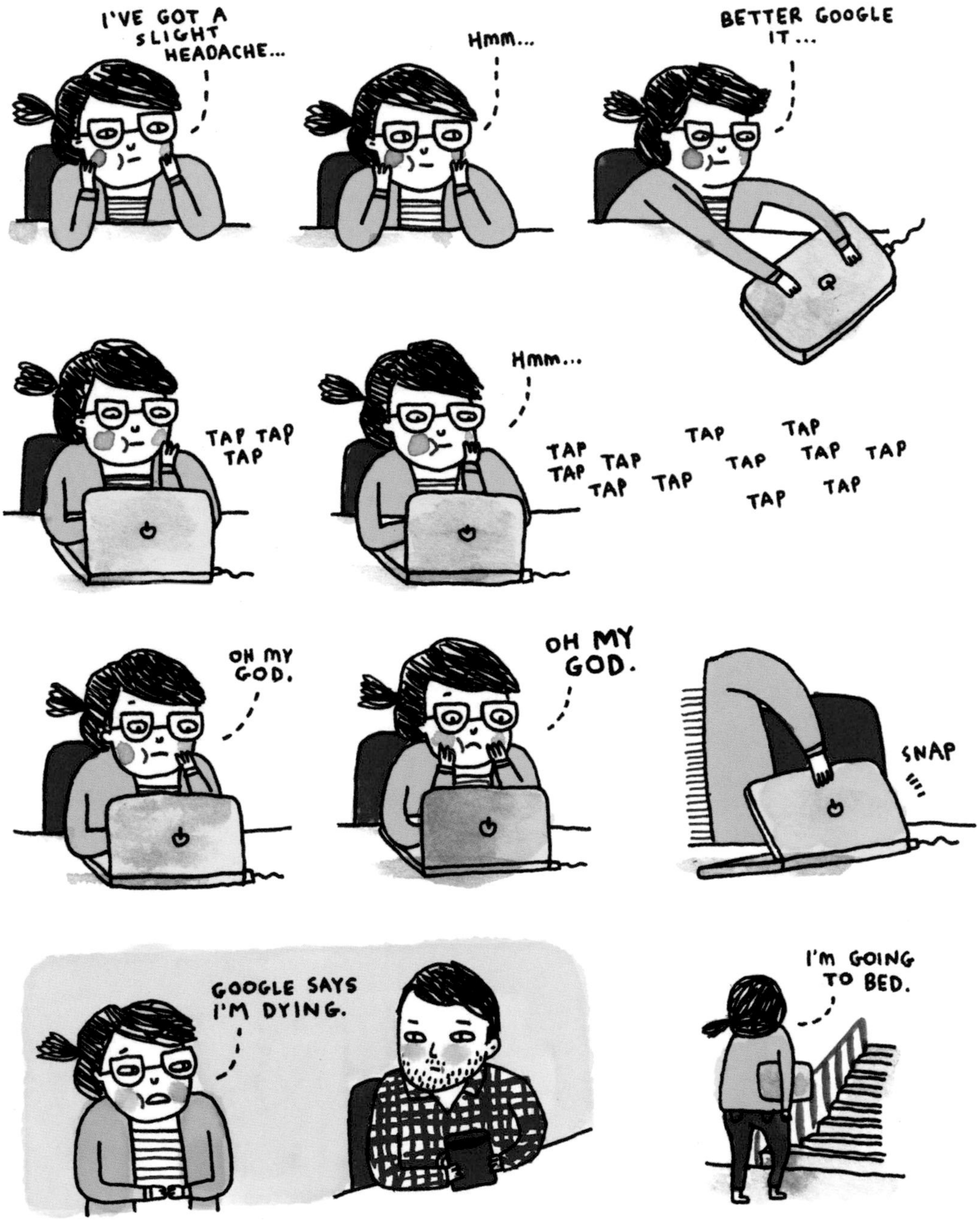
I'VE GOT A SLIGHT HEADACHE...
Hmm...
BETTER GOOGLE IT...
TAP TAP TAP
Hmm...
TAP TAP TAP TAP TAP TAP TAP TAP TAP TAP TAP TAP
OH MY GOD.
OH MY GOD.
SNAP
GOOGLE SAYS I'M DYING.
I'M GOING TO BED.

NEW! THE DISEASE-A-DAY CALENDAR

THE PERFECT GIFT FOR THE HYPOCHONDRIAC IN *YOUR* LIFE!

- 365 DAYS OF MALADIES!
- FULL COLOR PHOTOS!
- IN-DEPTH DESCRIPTIONS!
- FREE APP DOWNLOAD!

only $13.99

LUMPY CUSTARD FOLIACEUS DISEASE

JAN 1

ANGRY BEAVER FEVER

JUL 6

BARISTA'S ELBOW

OCT 20

SMURF VIRUS

MAY 14

ORDER NOW AND GET A SET OF OUR "SKIN DISORDERS" PLAYING CARDS ABSOLUTELY FREE!

MEDITATION

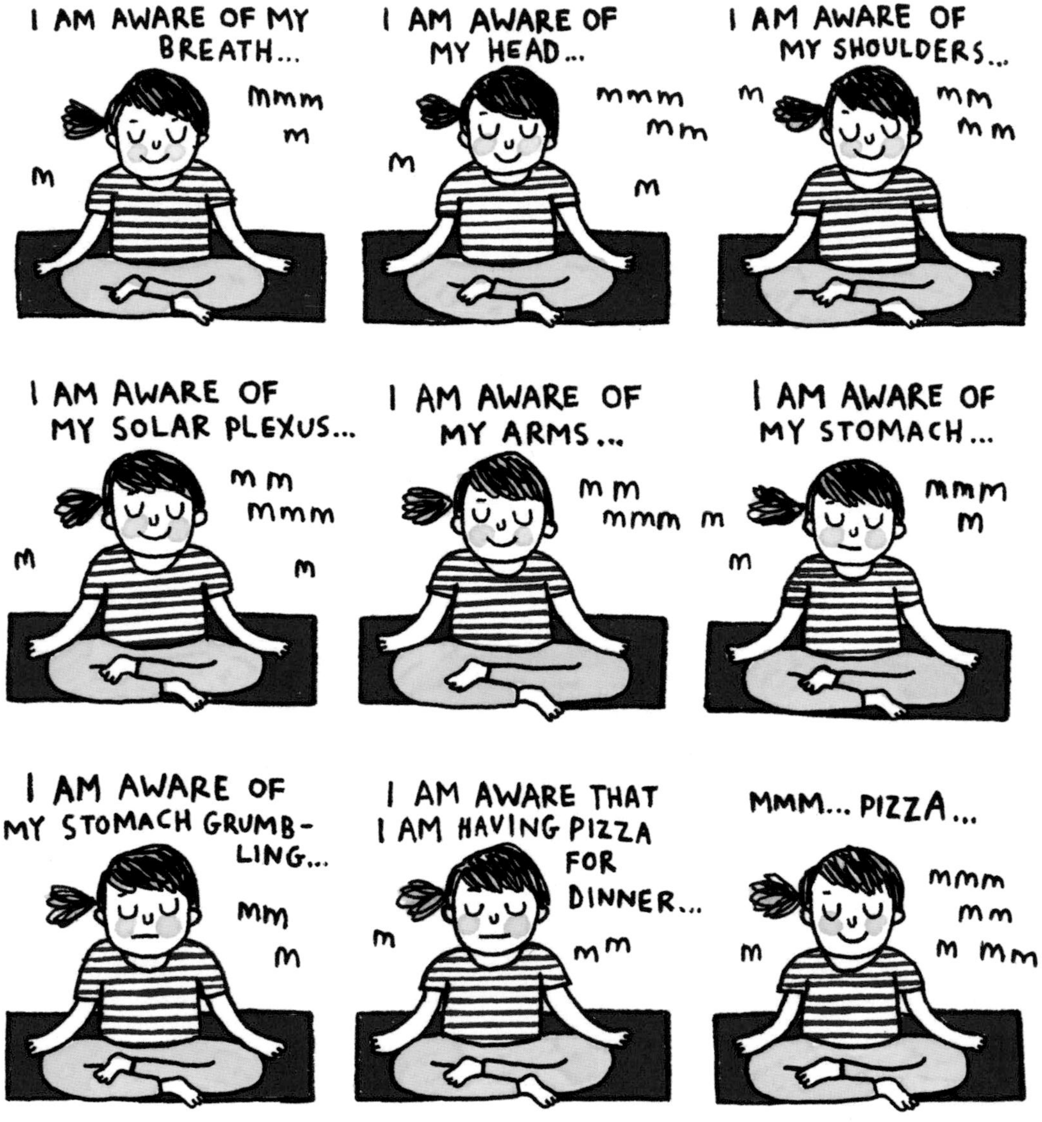
I AM AWARE OF MY BREATH...
mmm m m
I AM AWARE OF MY HEAD...
mmm mm m m
I AM AWARE OF MY SHOULDERS...
m mm mm
I AM AWARE OF MY SOLAR PLEXUS...
m m mmm m m
I AM AWARE OF MY ARMS...
m m mmm m
I AM AWARE OF MY STOMACH...
mmm m m
I AM AWARE OF MY STOMACH GRUMB-LING...
mm m
I AM AWARE THAT I AM HAVING PIZZA FOR DINNER...
m mm
MMM... PIZZA...
mmm mm m m mm

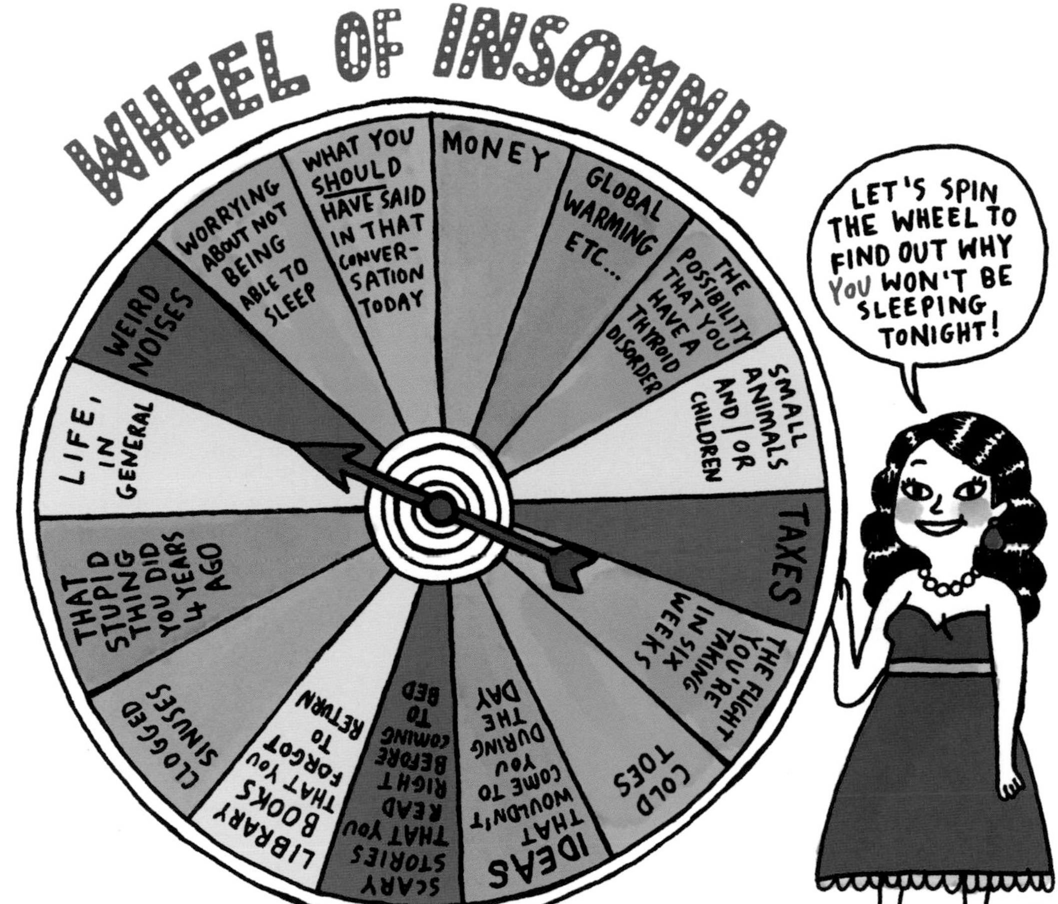
WHEEL OF INSOMNIA
WHAT YOU SHOULD HAVE SAID IN THAT CONVERSATION TODAY
MONEY
GLOBAL WARMING ETC...
THE POSSIBILITY THAT YOU HAVE A THYROID DISORDER
SMALL ANIMALS AND/OR CHILDREN
TAXES
THE FLIGHT YOU'RE TAKING IN SIX WEEKS
COLD TOES
IDEAS THAT WOULDN'T COME TO YOU DURING THE DAY
SCARY STORIES THAT YOU READ RIGHT BEFORE COMING TO BED
LIBRARY BOOKS THAT YOU FORGOT TO RETURN
CLOGGED SINUSES
THAT STUPID THING YOU DID 4 YEARS AGO
LIFE, IN GENERAL
WEIRD NOISES
WORRYING ABOUT NOT BEING ABLE TO SLEEP
LET'S SPIN THE WHEEL TO FIND OUT WHY YOU WON'T BE SLEEPING TONIGHT!

WHAT GYM ADS, WOMEN'S MAGAZINES, AND GOOGLE IMAGE SEARCH THINK A "WOMAN EXERCISING" LOOKS LIKE

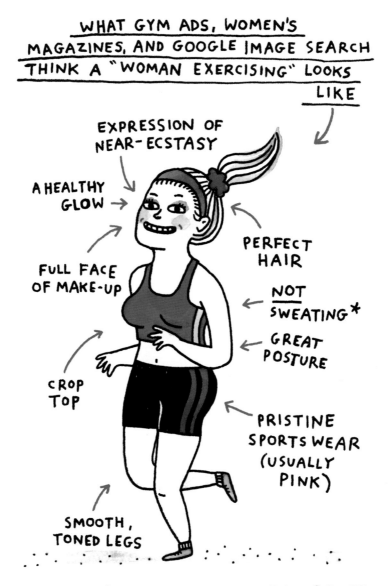

EXPRESSION OF NEAR-ECSTASY

A HEALTHY GLOW →

PERFECT HAIR

FULL FACE OF MAKE-UP

← NOT SWEATING *

← GREAT POSTURE

CROP TOP

← PRISTINE SPORTS WEAR (USUALLY PINK)

SMOOTH, TONED LEGS

* "HORSES SWEAT, MEN PERSPIRE, AND YOUNG LADIES GET IN A GLOW."
The Medical Age, 1883

WHAT I LOOK LIKE
WHEN EXERCISING

EXPRESSION OF
SHEER DESPAIR

A DEATHLY
PALLOR →

GLASSES
SLIPPING
DOWN
NOSE

HAIR JUST
IN USUAL STATE
BUT NOW ALSO
SWEATY

SWEATING
LIKE A
SWEATY PIG*

WHICHEVER
BAGGY OLD
T-SHIRT I
FOUND ON
THE FLOOR

HOLEY
OLD
JOGGERS
(OR LEGGINGS)

*OR, A HORSE

LEGS ARE NEITHER
SMOOTH NOR TONED, BELIEVE ME.

THOUGHTS DURING YOGA RELAXATION

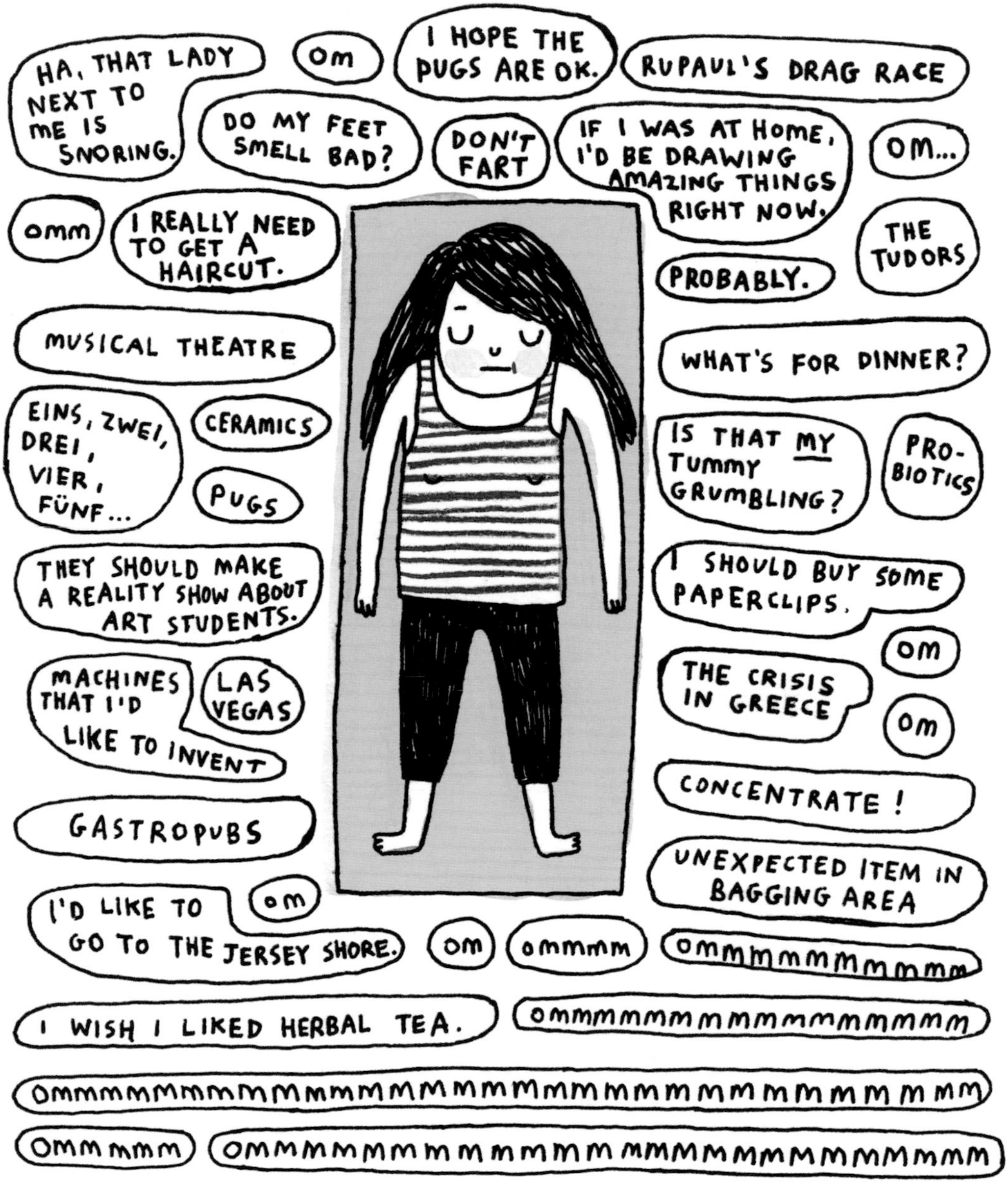
HA, THAT LADY NEXT TO ME IS SNORING.
OM
I HOPE THE PUGS ARE OK.
RUPAUL'S DRAG RACE
DO MY FEET SMELL BAD?
DON'T FART
IF I WAS AT HOME, I'D BE DRAWING AMAZING THINGS RIGHT NOW.
OM...
OMM
I REALLY NEED TO GET A HAIRCUT.
PROBABLY.
THE TUDORS
MUSICAL THEATRE
WHAT'S FOR DINNER?
EINS, ZWEI, DREI, VIER, FÜNF...
CERAMICS
PUGS
IS THAT MY TUMMY GRUMBLING?
PRO-BIOTICS
THEY SHOULD MAKE A REALITY SHOW ABOUT ART STUDENTS.
I SHOULD BUY SOME PAPERCLIPS.
MACHINES THAT I'D LIKE TO INVENT
LAS VEGAS
OM
THE CRISIS IN GREECE
OM
CONCENTRATE!
GASTROPUBS
UNEXPECTED ITEM IN BAGGING AREA
I'D LIKE TO GO TO THE JERSEY SHORE.
OM
OM
OMMMM
OMMMMMMMMMMM
I WISH I LIKED HERBAL TEA.
OMMMMMMMMMMMMMMMMMMM
OMMMMMMMMMMMMMMMMMMMMMMMMMMMMMMM
OMMMMM
OMMMMMMMMMMMMMMMMMMMMMMMMMMMM

EXERCISE FOR BETTER MENTAL HEALTH... WITH YOUR PETS!

DOGA

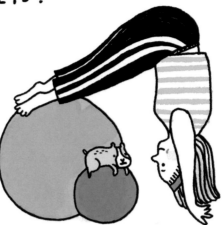

GUINEA PIG-LATES

T'AI CHINCHILLA

JUST SITTING DOWN AND HAVING A REALLY GOOD CHAT WITH YOUR CAT

CHAPTER TWO

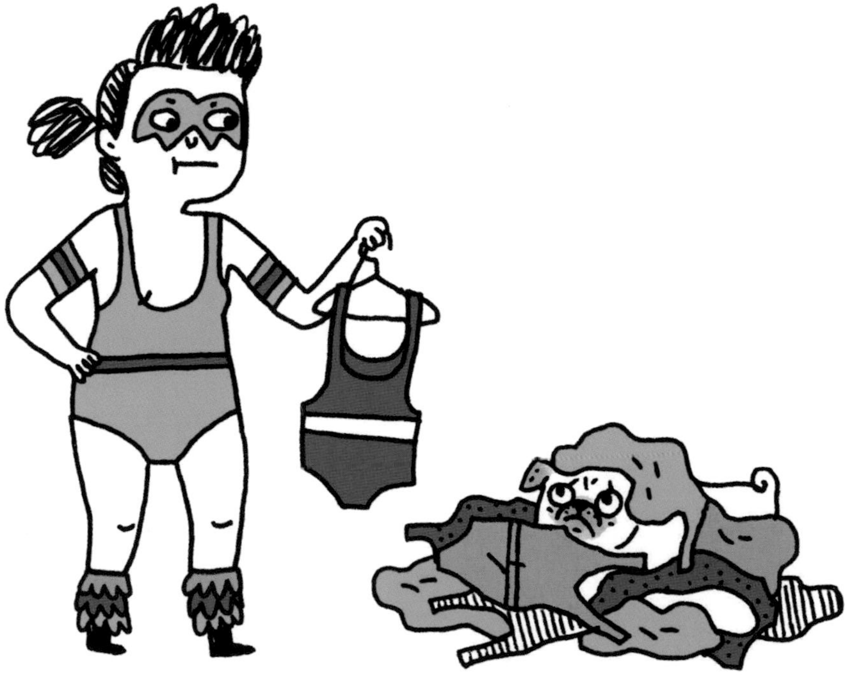

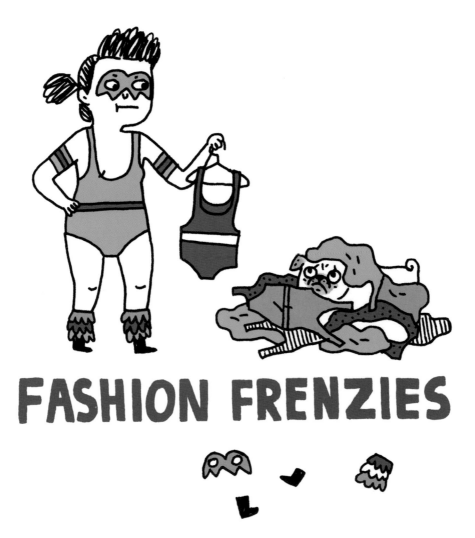

FASHION FRENZIES

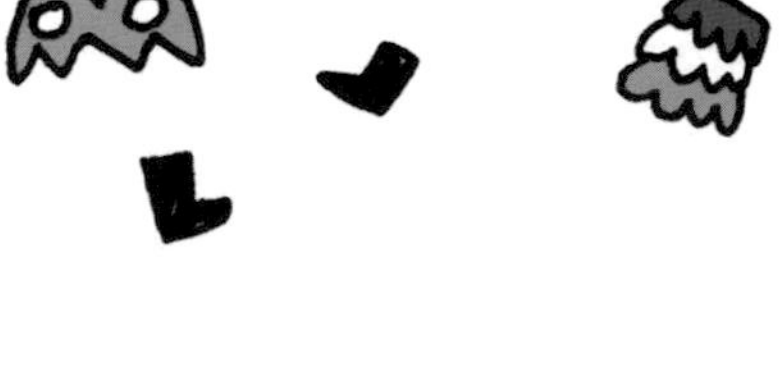

HOT NEW EYE MAKE-UP LOOKS!

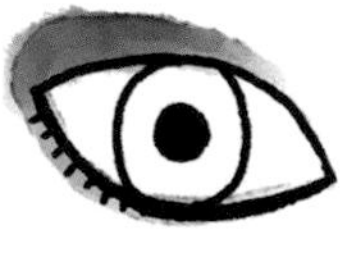

SMOKY EYE

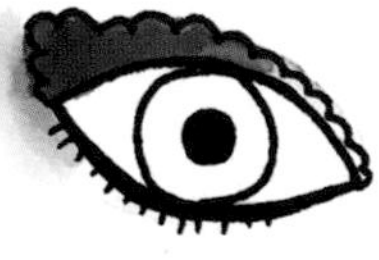

FOGGY EYE

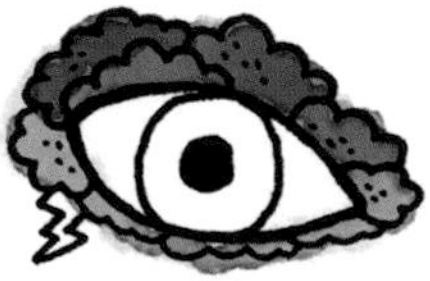

STORMY EYE

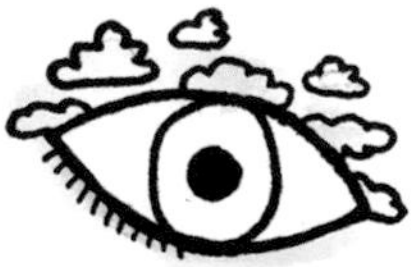

CLOUDY EYE WITH A 40% CHANCE OF RAIN

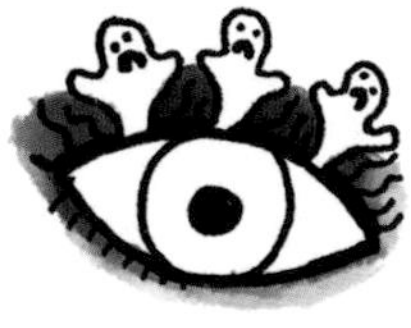

SPOOKY EYE

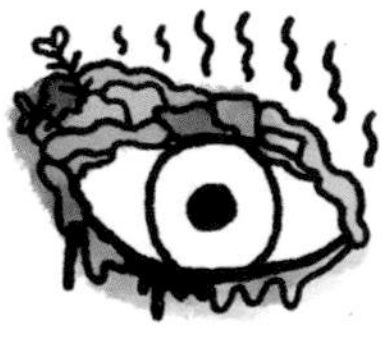

STINKY EYE

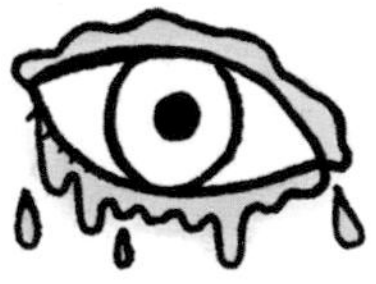

SOGGY EYE

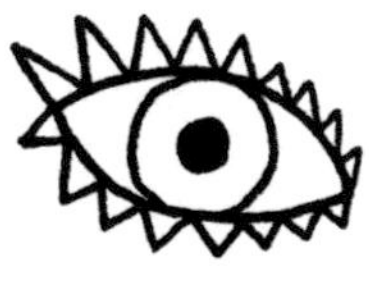

SPIKY EYE

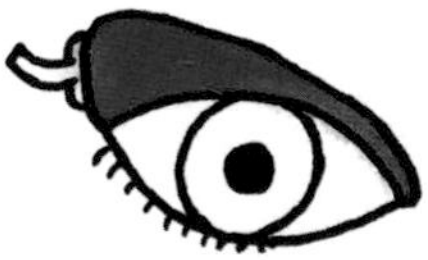

SPICY EYE

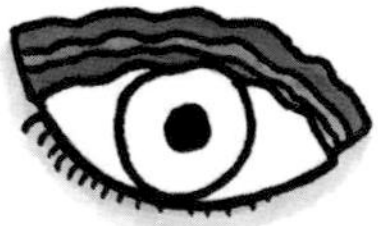

SMOKY BACON EYE

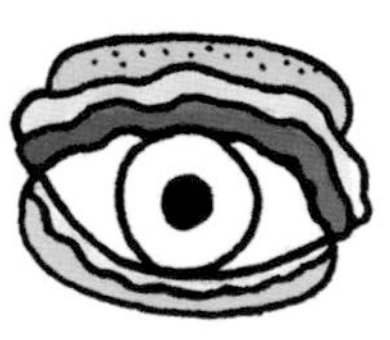

SMOKED SALMON BAGEL EYE

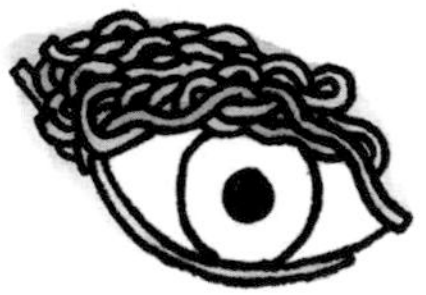

SPAGHETTI EYE

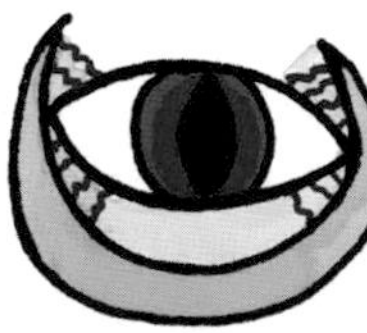

EYE OF SAURON

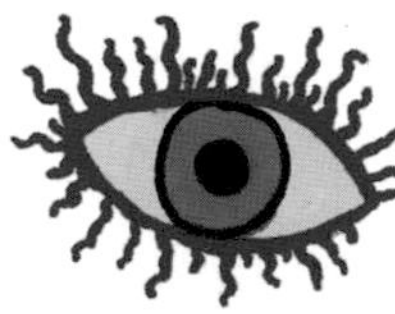

EYE OF CTHULHU

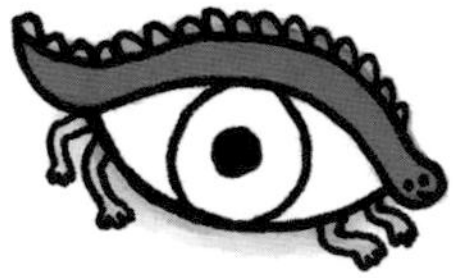

EYE OF NEWT

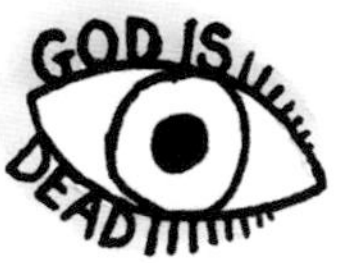
GOD IS
DEAD

EYE OF NIETZSCHE

HIGHLIGHTS FROM THE NEW

SEPHORROR
CATALOG

EVERLASTING LIP COLOR THAT WILL NEVER FADE! (NEITHER WILL THE CURSE.)

Stretch Extreme MASCARA

USES ACTUAL MEDIEVAL TORTURE METHODS TO LENGTHEN YOUR LASHES!

Evil Eye SHADOW

CONTAINS PORTAL TO HELL AND ALSO, GLITTER.

D. GRAY'S
Age Defying
MOISTURIZER

FOR ETERNALLY* YOUTHFUL SKIN

*FULL EFFECTIVENESS MAY REQUIRE PACT WITH THE DEVIL

URBAN BIRTHSTONES

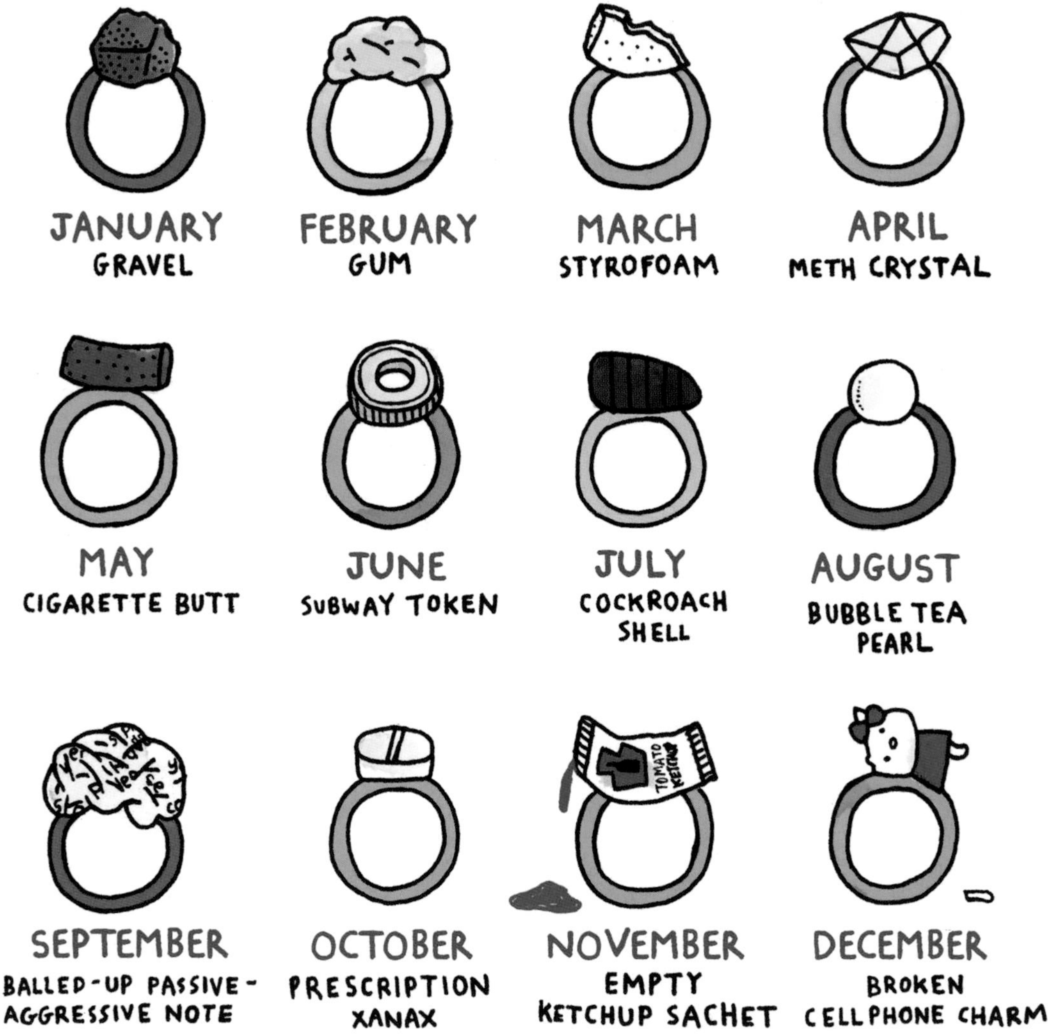
JANUARY
GRAVEL
FEBRUARY
GUM
MARCH
STYROFOAM
APRIL
METH CRYSTAL
MAY
CIGARETTE BUTT
JUNE
SUBWAY TOKEN
JULY
COCKROACH SHELL
AUGUST
BUBBLE TEA PEARL
SEPTEMBER
BALLED-UP PASSIVE-AGGRESSIVE NOTE
OCTOBER
PRESCRIPTION XANAX
NOVEMBER
EMPTY KETCHUP SACHET
TOMATO KETCHUP
DECEMBER
BROKEN CELLPHONE CHARM

LESS POPULAR NAIL POLISH COLORS

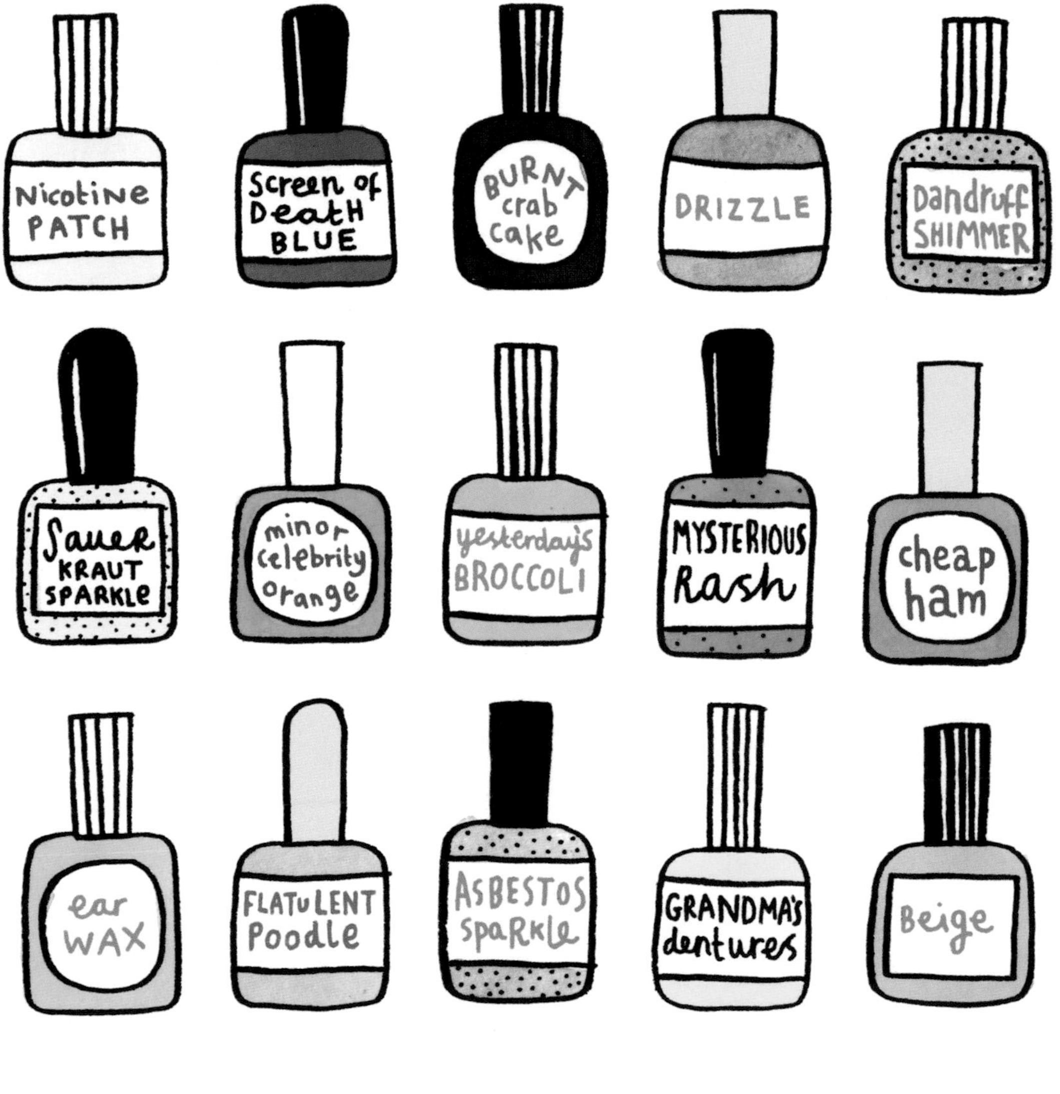
Nicotine PATCH
Screen of Death BLUE
BURNT crab cake
DRIZZLE
Dandruff SHIMMER
Sauer KRAUT SPARKLE
minor celebrity orange
yesterday's BROCCOLI
MYSTERIOUS Rash
cheap ham
ear WAX
FLATULENT Poodle
ASBESTOS sparkle
GRANDMA's dentures
Beige

HAIRSTYLES FOR THE FASHIONABLE YOUNG LADY

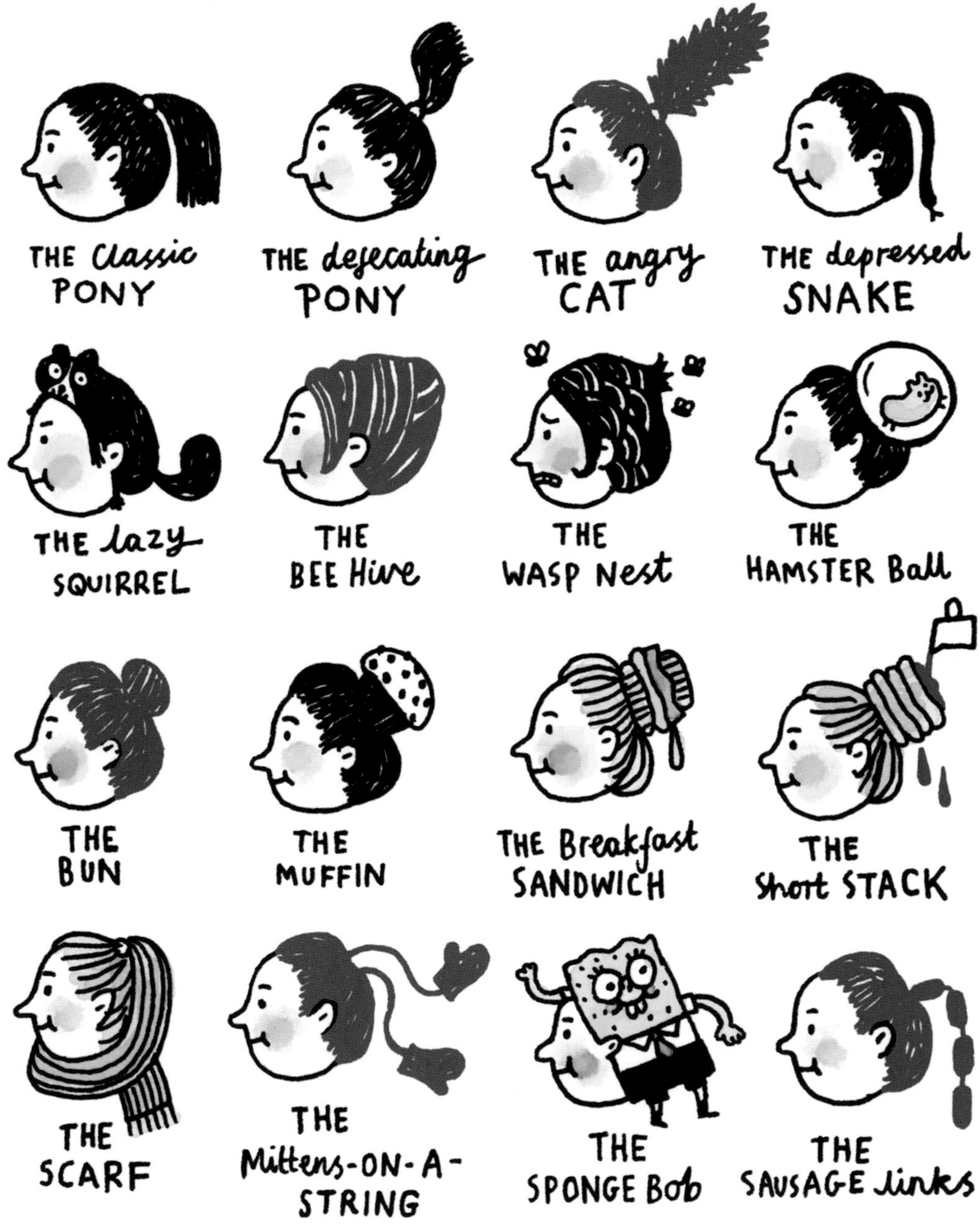
THE Classic PONY
THE defecating PONY
THE angry CAT
THE depressed SNAKE
THE lazy SQUIRREL
THE BEE Hive
THE WASP Nest
THE HAMSTER Ball
THE BUN
THE MUFFIN
THE Breakfast SANDWICH
THE Short STACK
THE SCARF
THE Mittens-ON-A-STRING
THE SPONGE Bob
THE SAUSAGE links

MORE DAIRY-BASED FACIAL HAIR STYLES

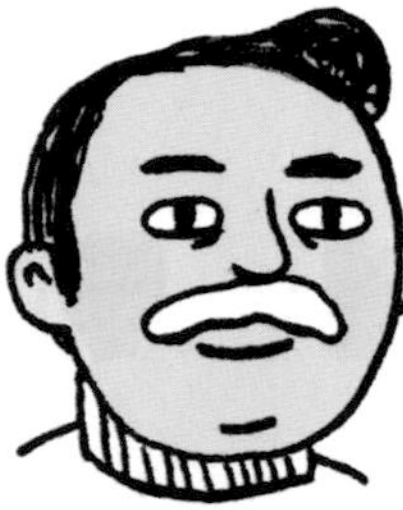
MILK MOUSTACHE

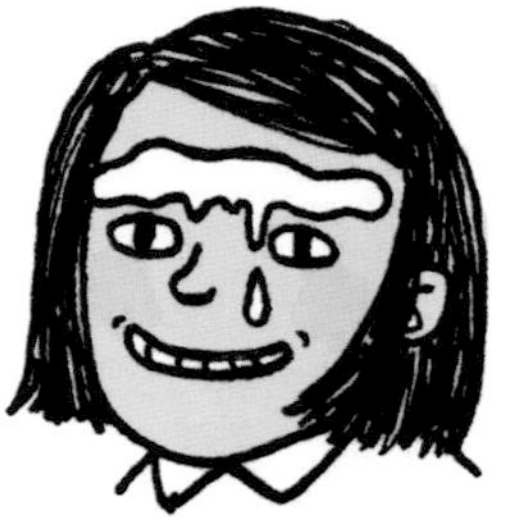
YOGURT UNI BROW

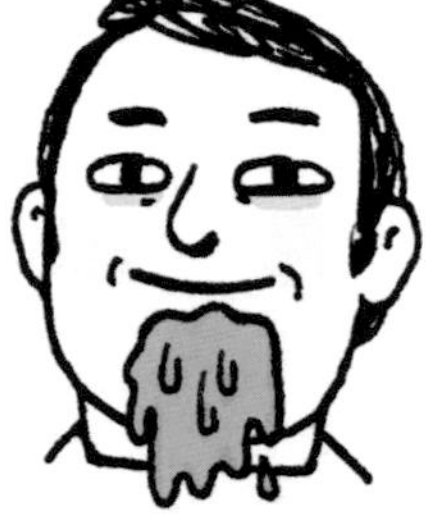
CUSTARD GOATEE

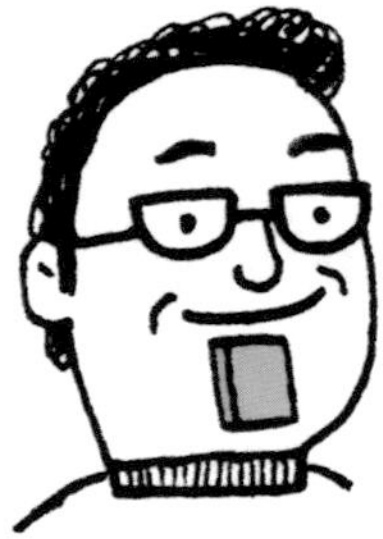
PAT O' BUTTER SOUL PATCH

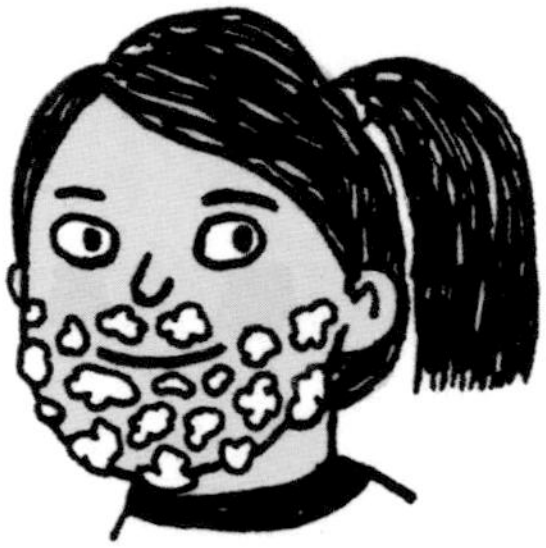
COTTAGE CHEESE STUBBLE

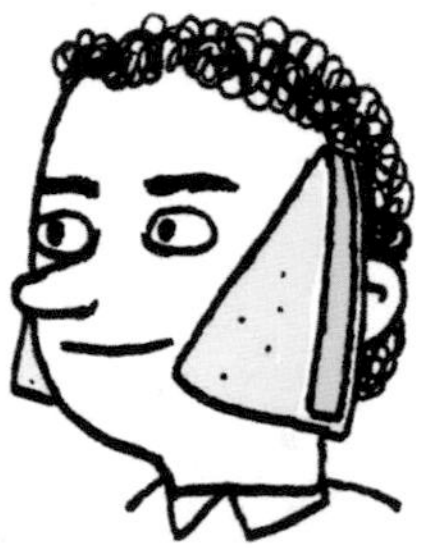
FRENCH BRIE MUTTON CHOPS

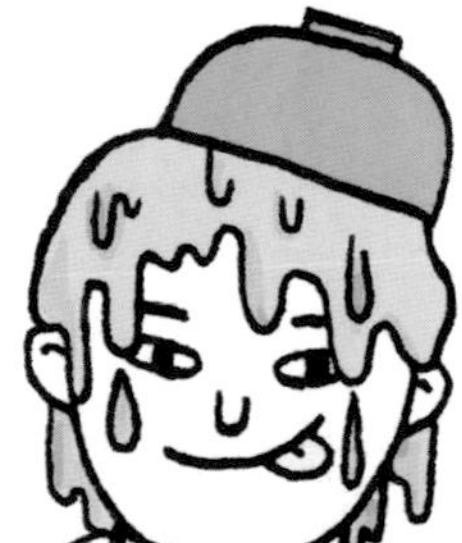
ICE CREAM BOWL CUT

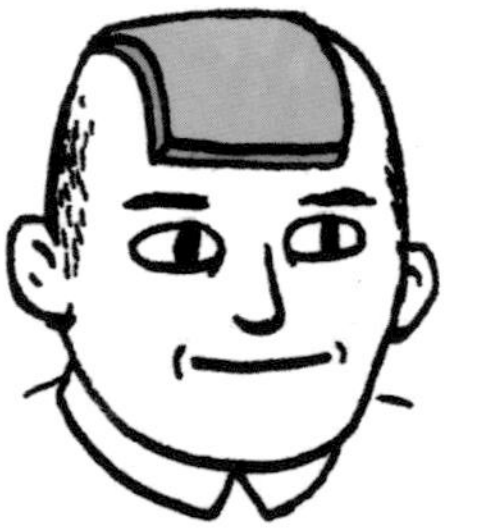
AMERICAN CHEESE TOUPÉE

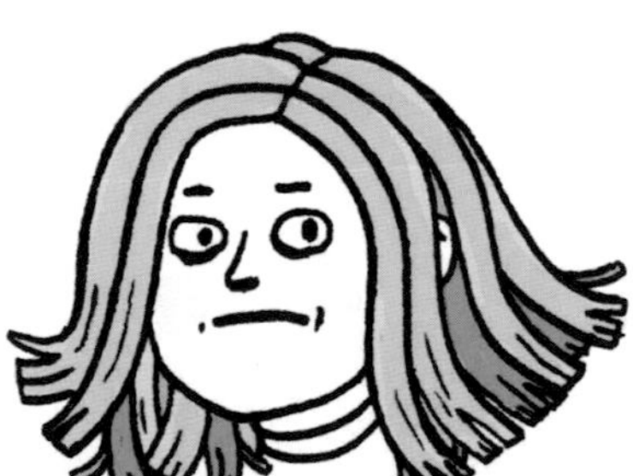
CHEESE STRING DREADLOCKS

THE ARCHAEOLOGY OF A PURSE

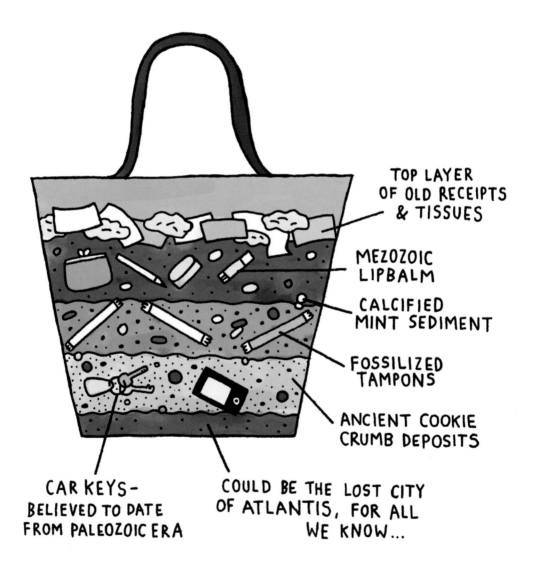

TOP LAYER
OF OLD RECEIPTS
& TISSUES

MEZOZOIC
LIPBALM

CALCIFIED
MINT SEDIMENT

FOSSILIZED
TAMPONS

ANCIENT COOKIE
CRUMB DEPOSITS

CAR KEYS-
BELIEVED TO DATE
FROM PALEOZOIC ERA

COULD BE THE LOST CITY
OF ATLANTIS, FOR ALL
WE KNOW...

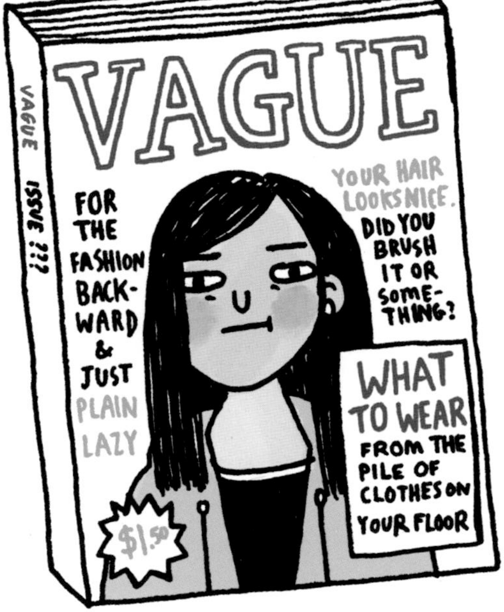
VAGUE
VAGUE
ISSUE ???
FOR THE FASHION BACKWARD & JUST PLAIN LAZY
YOUR HAIR LOOKS NICE. DID YOU BRUSH IT OR SOMETHING?
WHAT TO WEAR FROM THE PILE OF CLOTHES ON YOUR FLOOR
$1.50

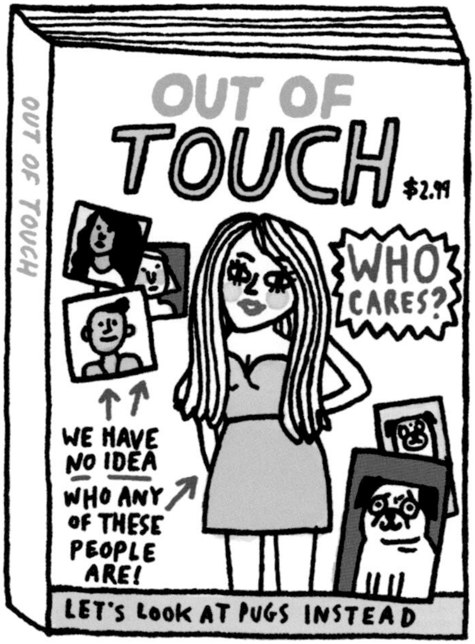
OUT OF TOUCH
OUT OF TOUCH
$2.99
WHO CARES?
WE HAVE NO IDEA WHO ANY OF THESE PEOPLE ARE!
LET'S LOOK AT PUGS INSTEAD

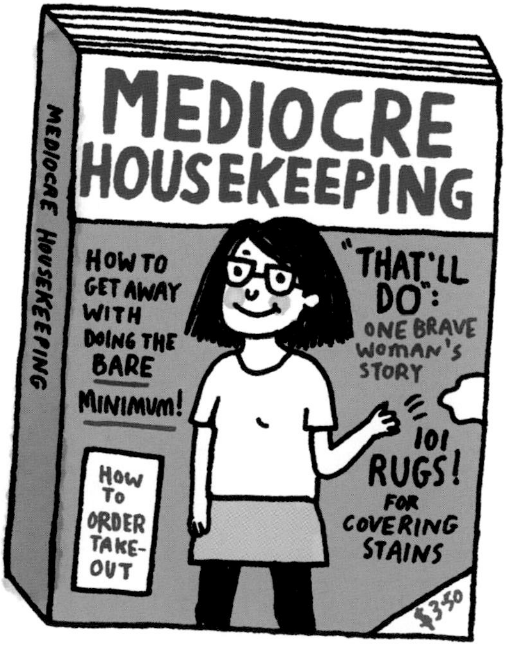
MEDIOCRE HOUSEKEEPING
MEDIOCRE HOUSEKEEPING
HOW TO GET AWAY WITH DOING THE BARE MINIMUM!
"THAT'LL DO": ONE BRAVE WOMAN'S STORY
101 RUGS! FOR COVERING STAINS
HOW TO ORDER TAKE-OUT
$3.50

MAKE YOUR OWN COUTURE HAT!

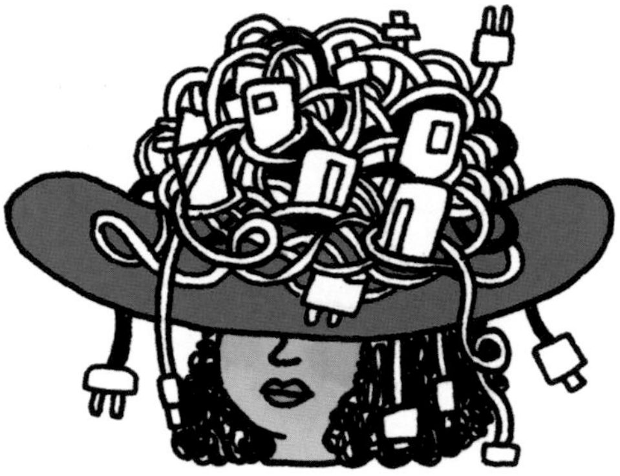

OLD CELLPHONE CHARGERS
AND DISCARDED SUPERMARKET
LOYALTY CARDS

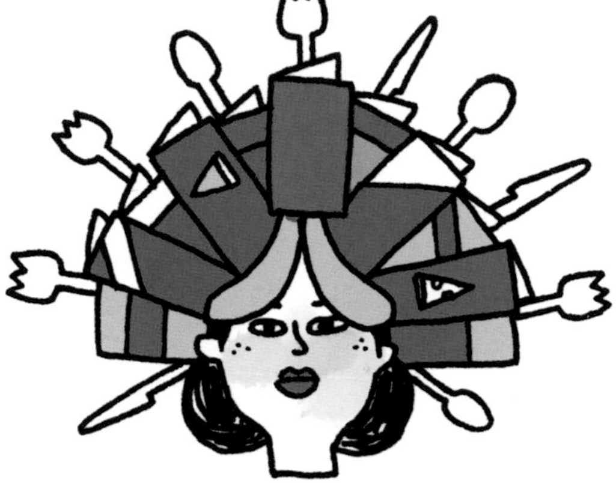

SEVERAL TAKE-OUT MENUS
AND SOME PLASTIC UTENSILS
STOLEN FROM THE DELI

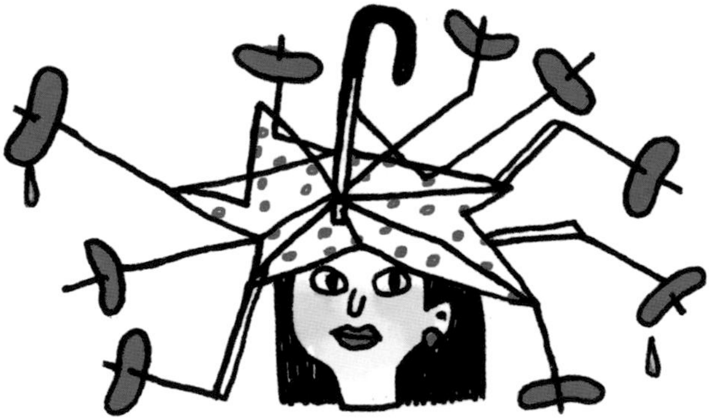

A DOLLAR STORE UMBRELLA
AND A PACK OF EXPIRED HOT DOGS

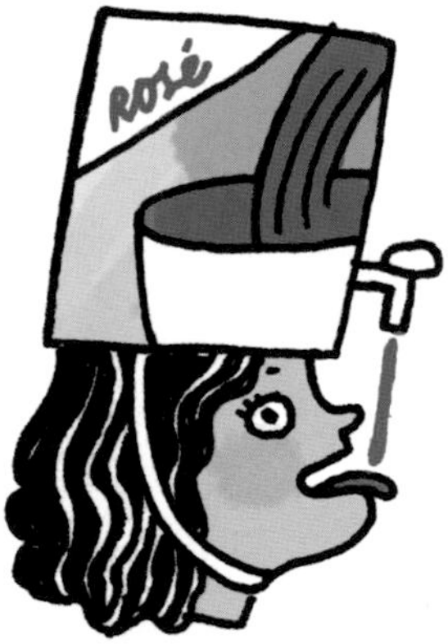
ROSÉ

A BOX OF WINE

NEW FAD DIETS

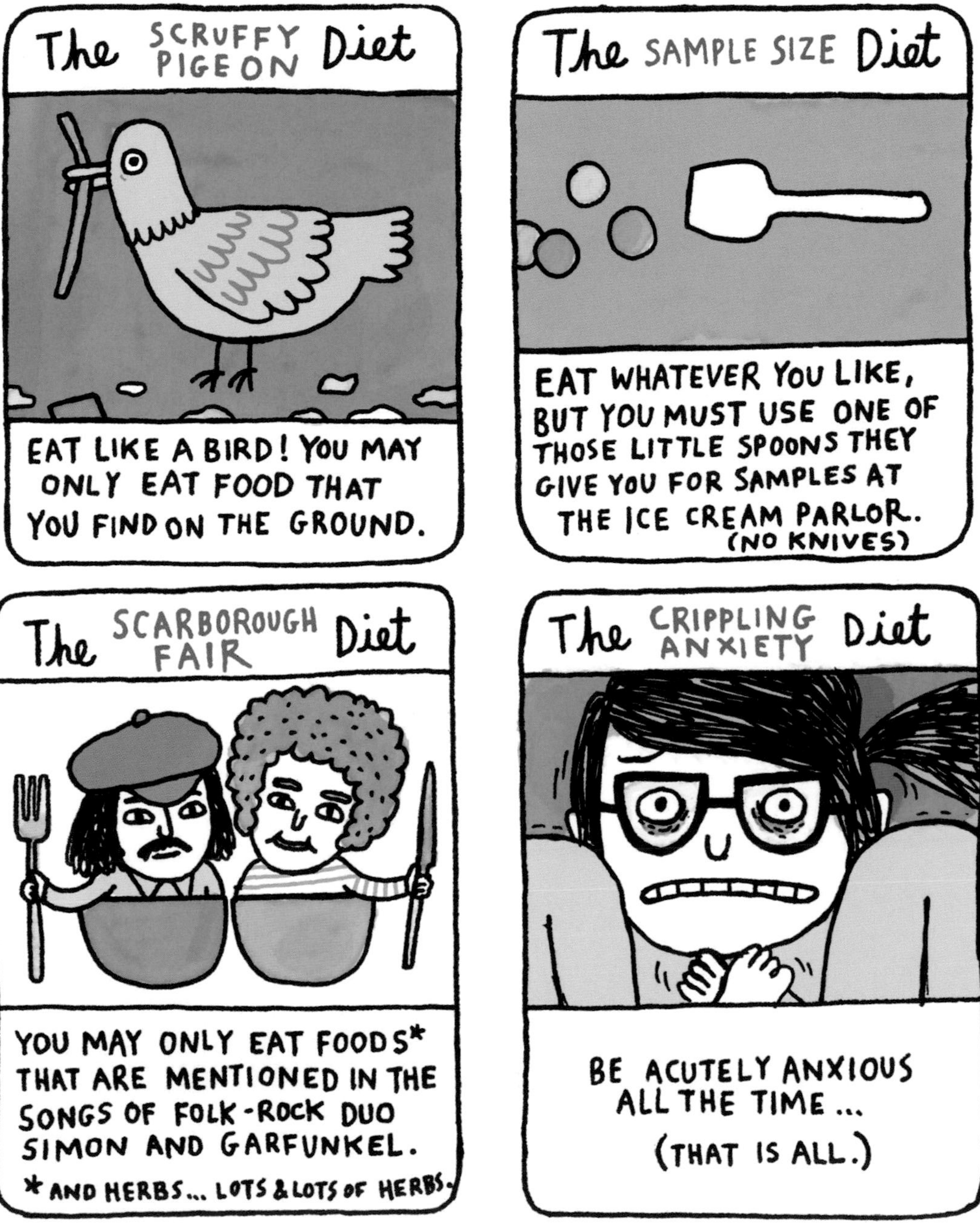
The SCRUFFY PIGEON Diet
EAT LIKE A BIRD! YOU MAY ONLY EAT FOOD THAT YOU FIND ON THE GROUND.
The SAMPLE SIZE Diet
EAT WHATEVER YOU LIKE, BUT YOU MUST USE ONE OF THOSE LITTLE SPOONS THEY GIVE YOU FOR SAMPLES AT THE ICE CREAM PARLOR.
(NO KNIVES)
The SCARBOROUGH FAIR Diet
YOU MAY ONLY EAT FOODS* THAT ARE MENTIONED IN THE SONGS OF FOLK-ROCK DUO SIMON AND GARFUNKEL.
* AND HERBS... LOTS & LOTS OF HERBS.
The CRIPPLING ANXIETY Diet
BE ACUTELY ANXIOUS ALL THE TIME...
(THAT IS ALL.)

STREET STYLE - FASHION WEEK SPECIAL

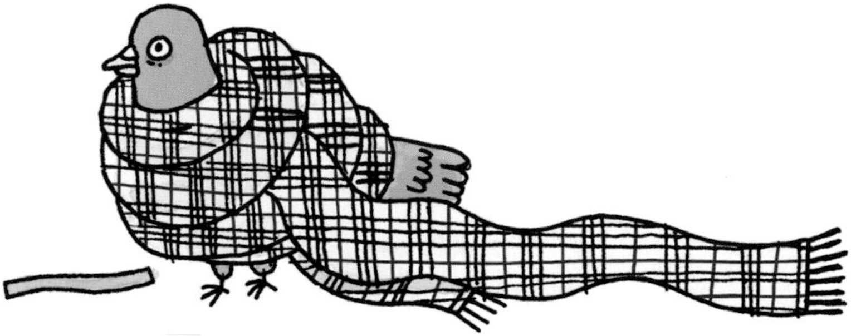

RACHEL, Pigeon
SCARF: Burberry
FRENCH FRY: Wendy's

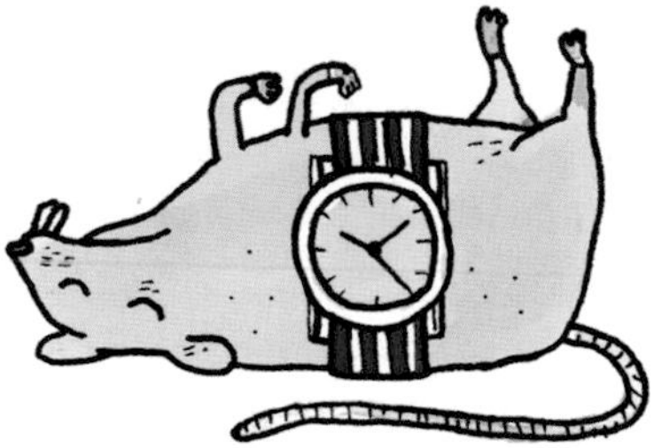

SARAH, dead rat
WATCH: Gucci
FLEAS: Sarah's own

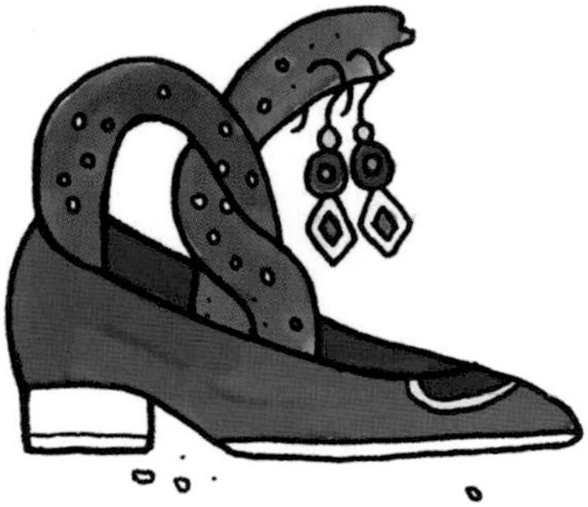

MOLLY, half-eaten pretzel
COURT SHOES: Charlotte Olympia
EARRINGS: vintage

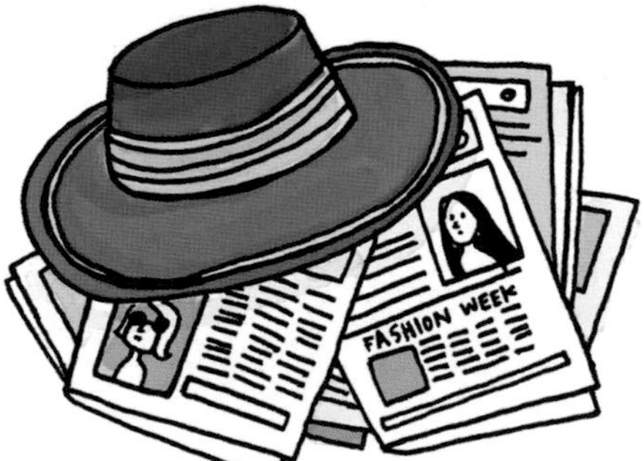
FASHION WEEK

JANET, pile of free newspapers
HAT: Stella McCartney

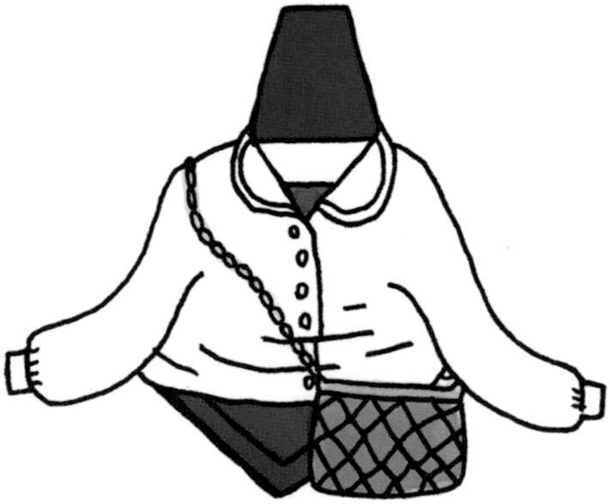

AMY, traffic cone
BLOUSE: Amy's own design
HANDBAG: Chanel

TREATMENTS AVAILABLE AT The British Spa™

The "SENSUOUS CUPPA" Massage

ENJOY THE CALMING SENSATION OF LUKEWARM TEA DRIPPING DOWN YOUR BACK, AS OUR EXPERT MASSEUSE KNEADS ALL OF YOUR TROUBLES AWAY, WHILE COMPLAINING ABOUT HER EX-BOYFRIEND.

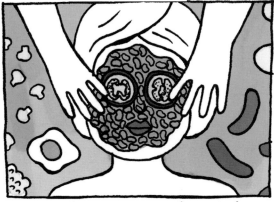

The "FULL ENGLISH" Facial

SIT BACK AND UNWIND AS WE SLATHER YOUR FACE WITH BAKED BEANS, EGGS, SAUSAGES, AND FRIED MUSHROOMS TO DRAW OUT TOXINS AND IMPURITIES. VEGETARIAN OPTION AVAILABLE.

The Pedicure "ROYALE"*

RELAX IN STYLE AS DOZENS OF CORGIS GENTLY NIBBLE AT THE HARD SKIN ON YOUR FEET, LEAVING THEM SMOOTH, SOFT, AND SMELLING FAINTLY OF KIBBLE.

I REALLY AM TERRIBLY SORRY.

The "POLITE" Bikini Wax

ALLOW US TO APOLOGIZE PROFUSELY WHILE WE VIOLENTLY YANK THE HAIR FROM YOUR MOST DELICATE REGIONS.

* DISCLAIMER: NOT ENDORSED BY HRH QUEEN ELIZABETH. MANAGEMENT RESERVES THE RIGHT TO REPLACE CORGIS WITH LABRADORS, CATS, OR BADGERS AT ANY TIME.

★★★ CHAPTER THREE ★★★

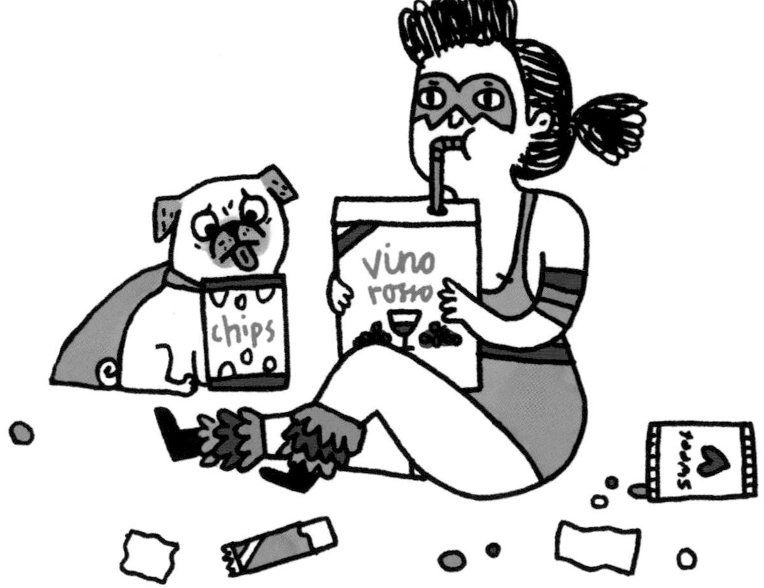
chips
vino
rosso

WHINING & DINING

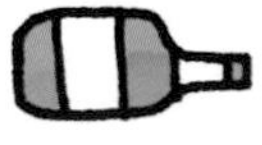

SPECIALITY COFFEE BEANS (THAT YOU SHOULD PROBABLY AVOID)

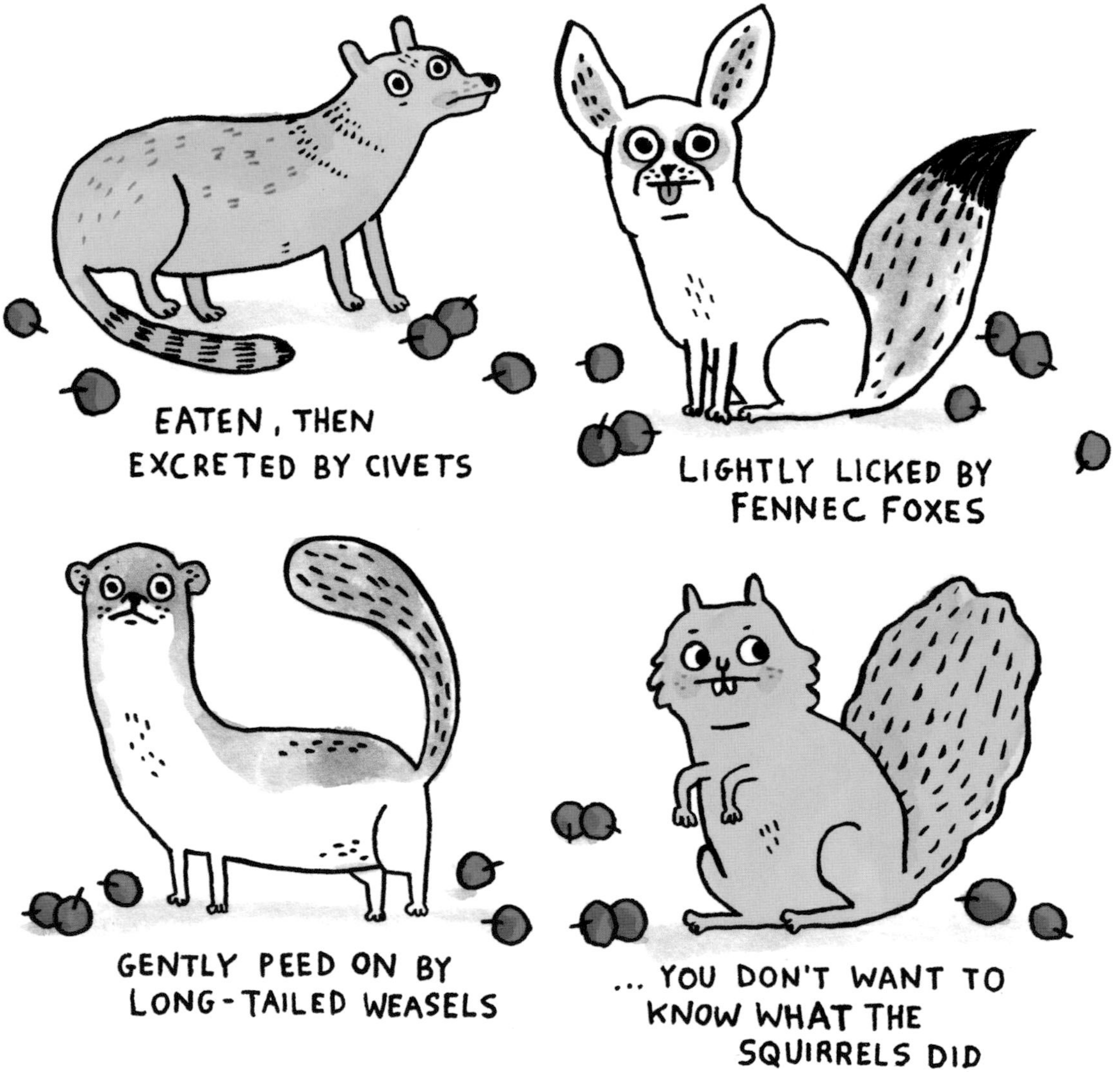
EATEN, THEN EXCRETED BY CIVETS
LIGHTLY LICKED BY FENNEC FOXES
GENTLY PEED ON BY LONG-TAILED WEASELS
... YOU DON'T WANT TO KNOW WHAT THE SQUIRRELS DID

DANGEROUS SEAFOOD

POISONOUS
PUFFER FISH

IMPROPERLY
COOKED SHELLFISH

LOBSTER THAT'S
LOOKING FOR TROUBLE

MOLLUSK GANG

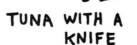

TUNA WITH A
KNIFE

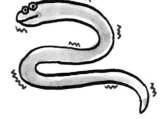

CLUMSY ELECTRIC EEL

SALMON THAT
HAS A BLACK BELT
IN KARATE

CAVIAR WITHOUT
A LICENSE

YOU'RE DUMB!

SQUID THAT'S JUST
REALLY MEAN

CAKES THAT ARE REALLY, REALLY BAD FOR YOU

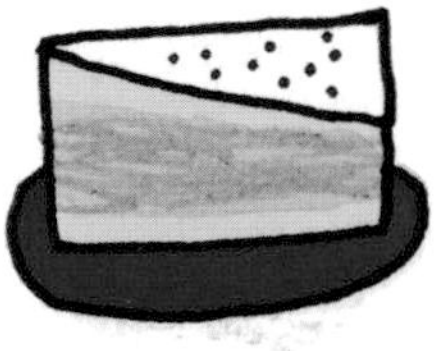

DEATH BY CHOCOLATE

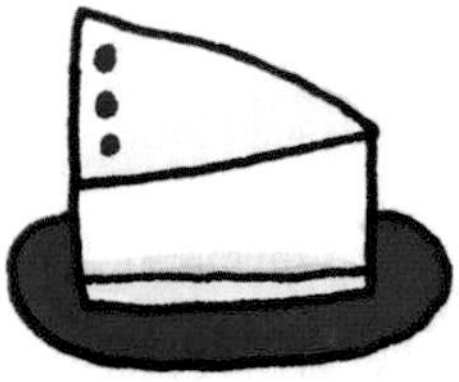

TUMMY ACHE BY LEMON

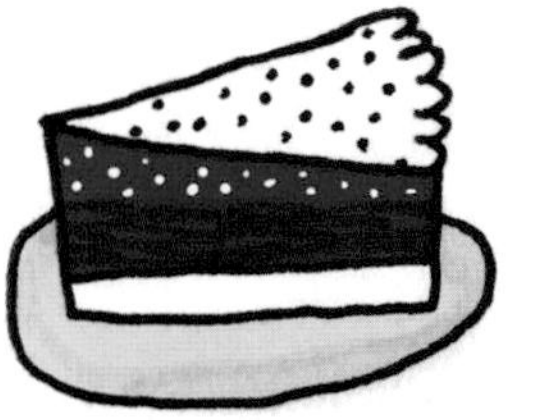

MIGRAINE BY GINGER

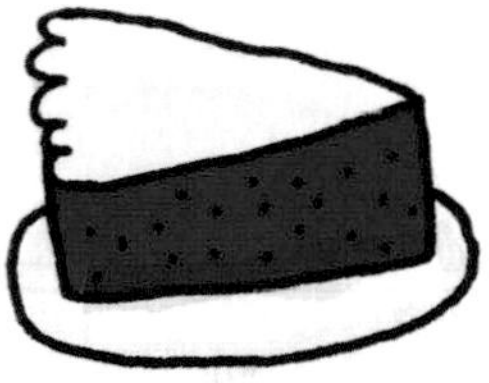

GLANDULAR FEVER BY CARROT, WITH A CREAM CHEESE FROSTING

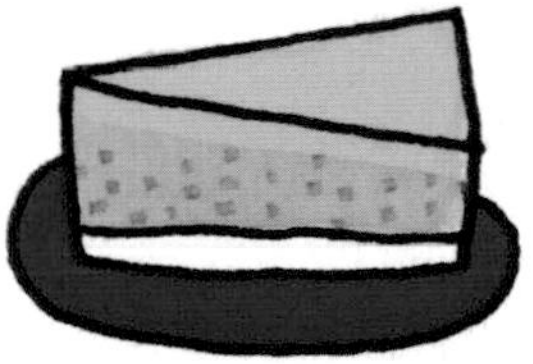

INFECTIOUS DISEASE BY CHERRY

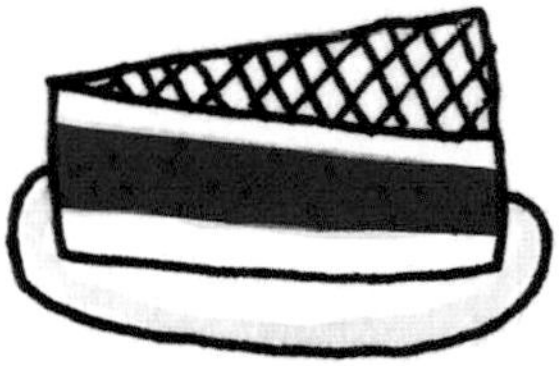

A NASTY CASE OF CYSTITIS BY RED VELVET

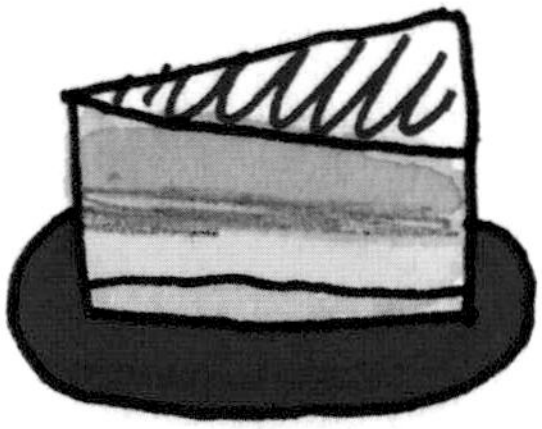

FLESH EATING VIRUS BY FUDGE

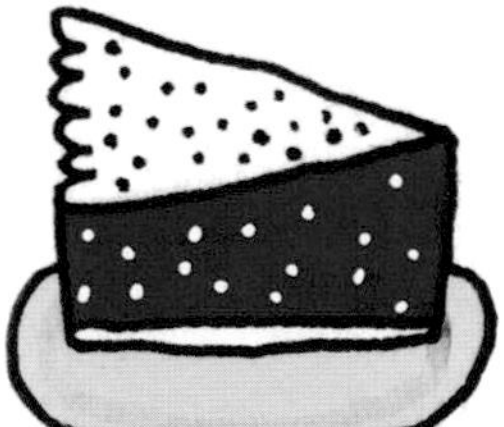

IT'S PROBABLY NOTHING, BUT YOU SHOULD GET IT CHECKED OUT ANYWAY BY ALMOND

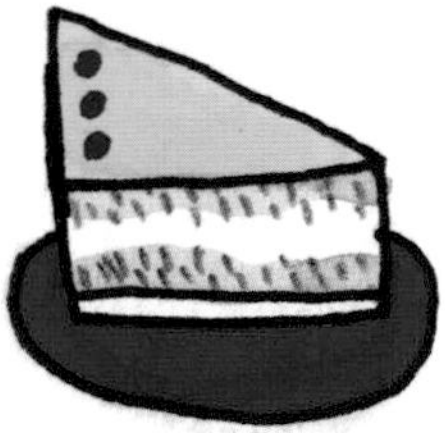

EMOTIONAL PROBLEMS BY APPLE

ICE CREAM FLAVORS FOR DESPERATE TIMES

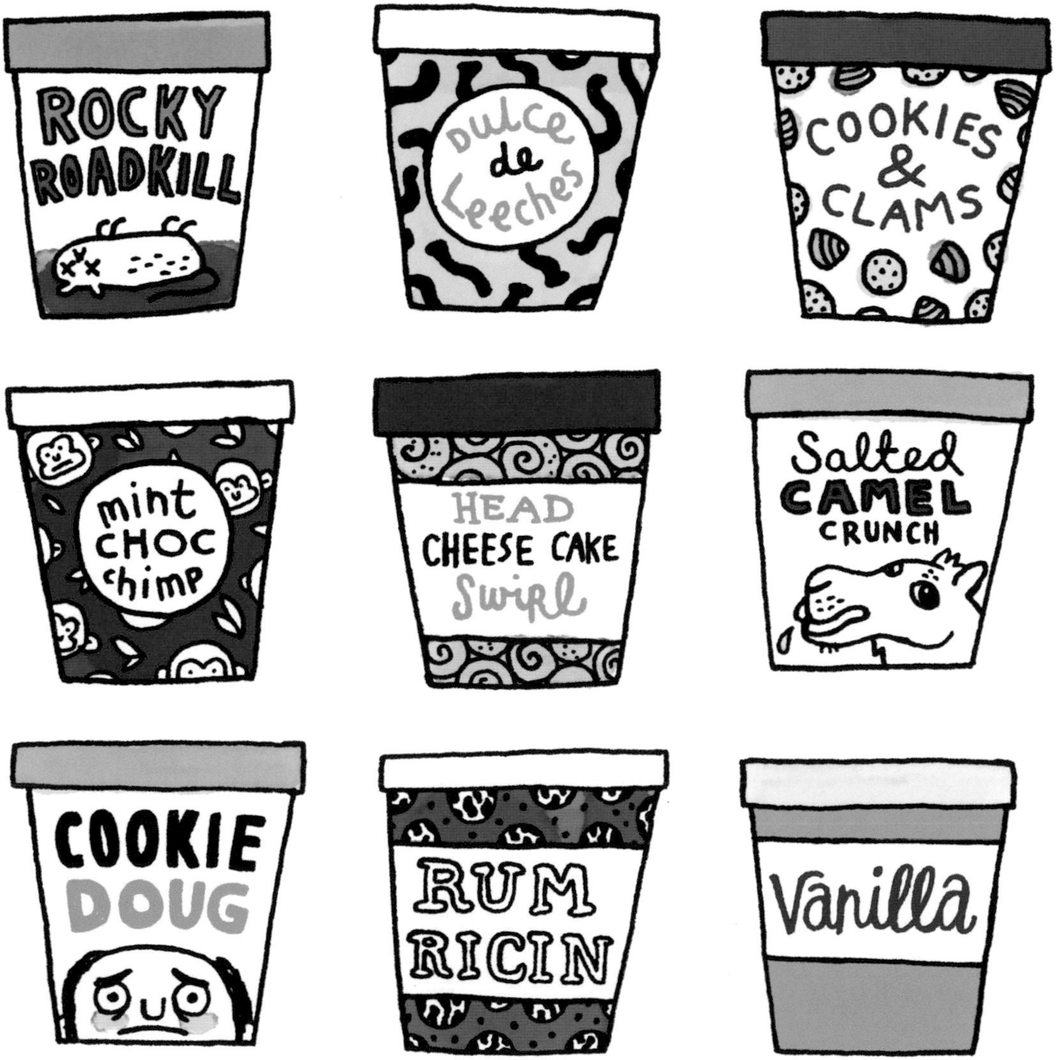
ROCKY ROADKILL
Dulce de Leeches
COOKIES & CLAMS
mint CHOC chimp
HEAD CHEESE CAKE Swirl
Salted CAMEL CRUNCH
COOKIE DOUG
RUM RICIN
Vanilla

PASTA SHAPES FOR THE DEPRESSED (translated from the original Italian)

"DOWNWARD SPIRALS"

"NERVOUS BUTTERFLIES"

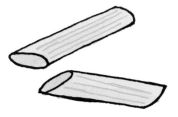

"MISERABLE TUBES"

"POINTLESS PIPES"

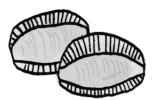

"EMPTY SHELLS"

"EXHAUSTED NOODLES"

"LITTLE PARCELS OF DESPAIR"

"DOWN-IN-THE DUMPLINGS"

"COMPLETELY FED-UP ALPHABETTI SPAGHETTI"

BAD GIRL SCOUT COOKIES

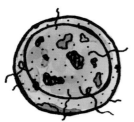

DRAG-A-LONGS

Lightly dusted with
lint and cat hair.

ASBESTOS DELITES

Laced with chocolate
chips and carcinogens.

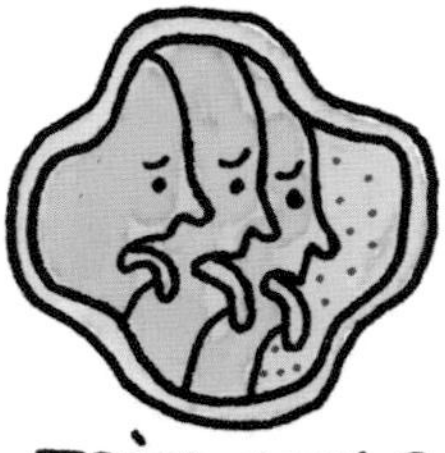

TRÈS FOULS

Dipped in something
unspeakably awful.

LEMON ACHES

Glazed with highly
corrosive citric acid.

TOOTH SNAPPERS

Chewy, with a solid
concrete center.

GOOD-FER-NOTHIN'S

Tasty, but also
exceedingly mean.

RADIOACTIVE MINTS

Gluten free, with a
glowing Uranium core.

SOYLENT CLUSTERS

Made with REAL
Boy Scouts!

MISERY CREMES

Filled with licorice
and existential dread.

EROTICA FOR FOODIES

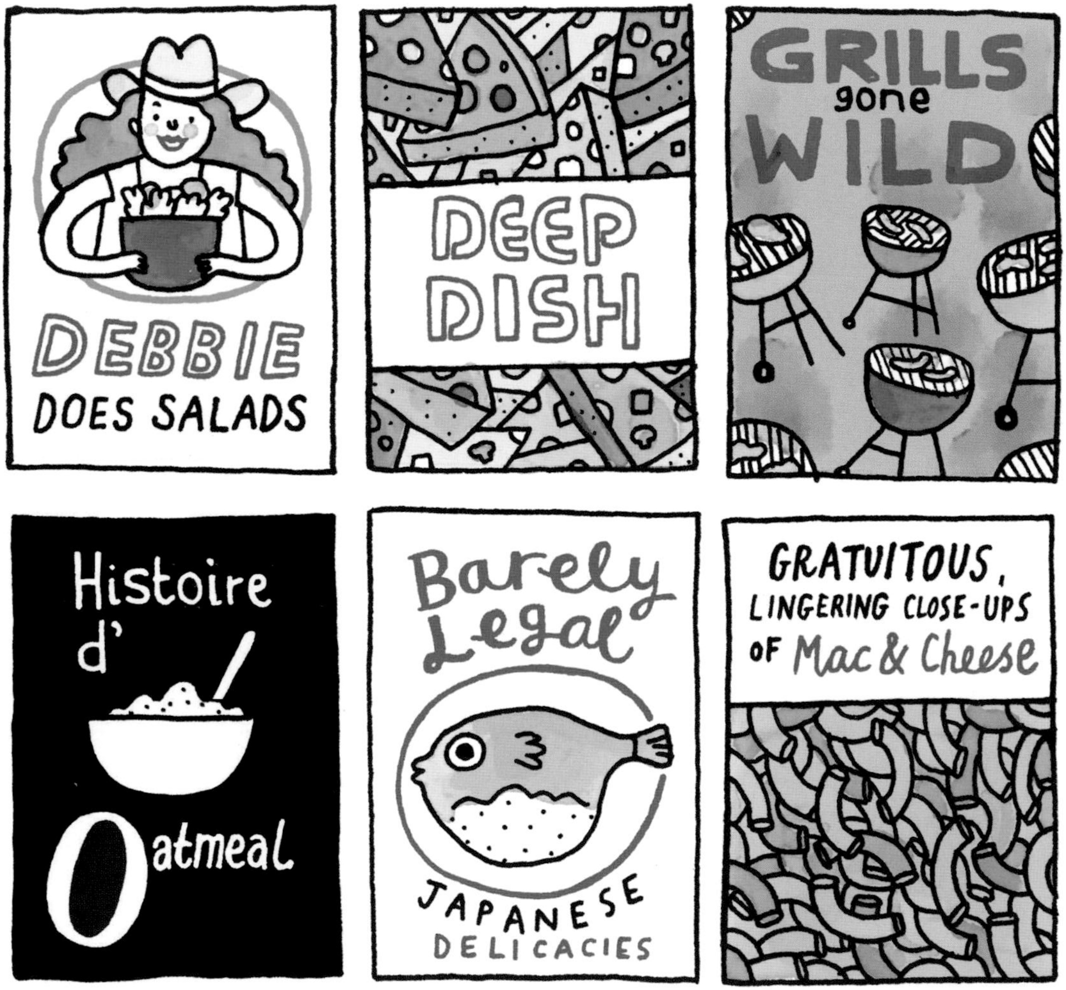
DEBBIE
DOES SALADS
DEEP DISH
GRILLS gone WILD
Histoire d' Oatmeal
Barely Legal
JAPANESE DELICACIES
GRATUITOUS, LINGERING CLOSE-UPS OF Mac & Cheese

INTRODUCING ... BREAKFAST PHARMACEREALS
THE GREAT NEW WAY TO TAKE YOUR MEDS!

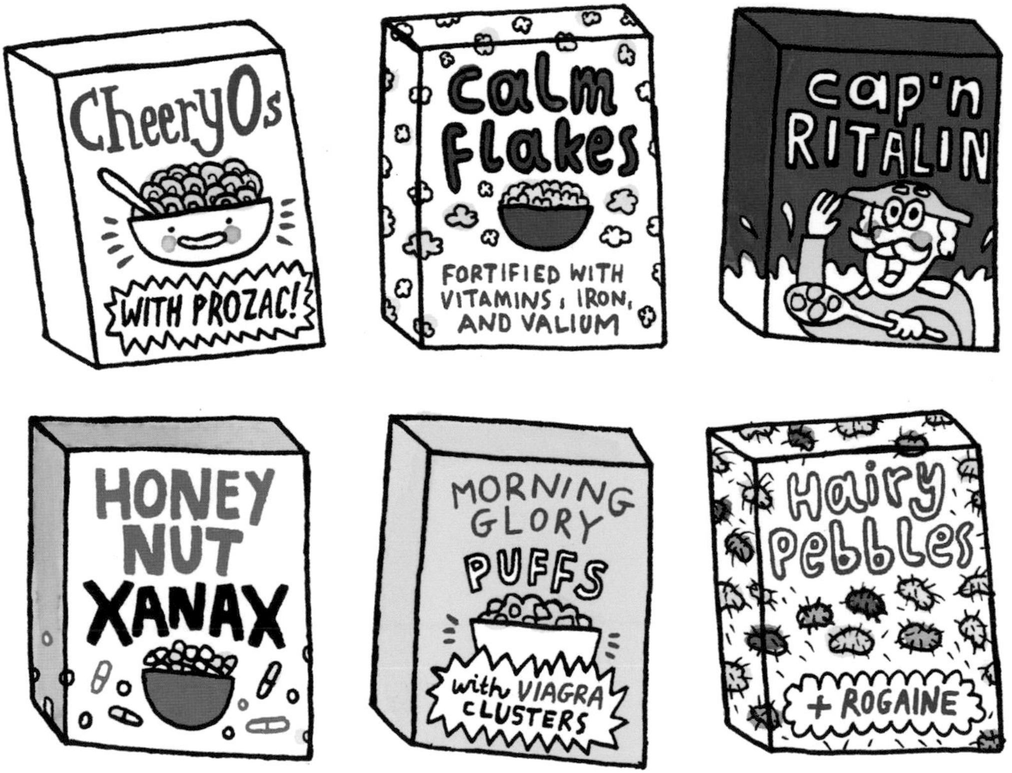
CheeryOs
WITH PROZAC!
Calm Flakes
FORTIFIED WITH VITAMINS, IRON, AND VALIUM
Cap'n RITALIN
HONEY NUT XANAX
MORNING GLORY PUFFS
with VIAGRA CLUSTERS
Hairy Pebbles
+ ROGAINE

CHAPTER FOUR

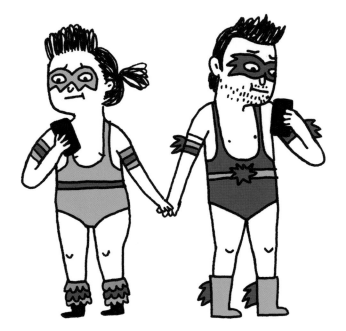

LOVE & OTHER ANXIETIES

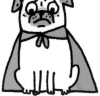

NON-COMMITAL VALENTINE CARDS

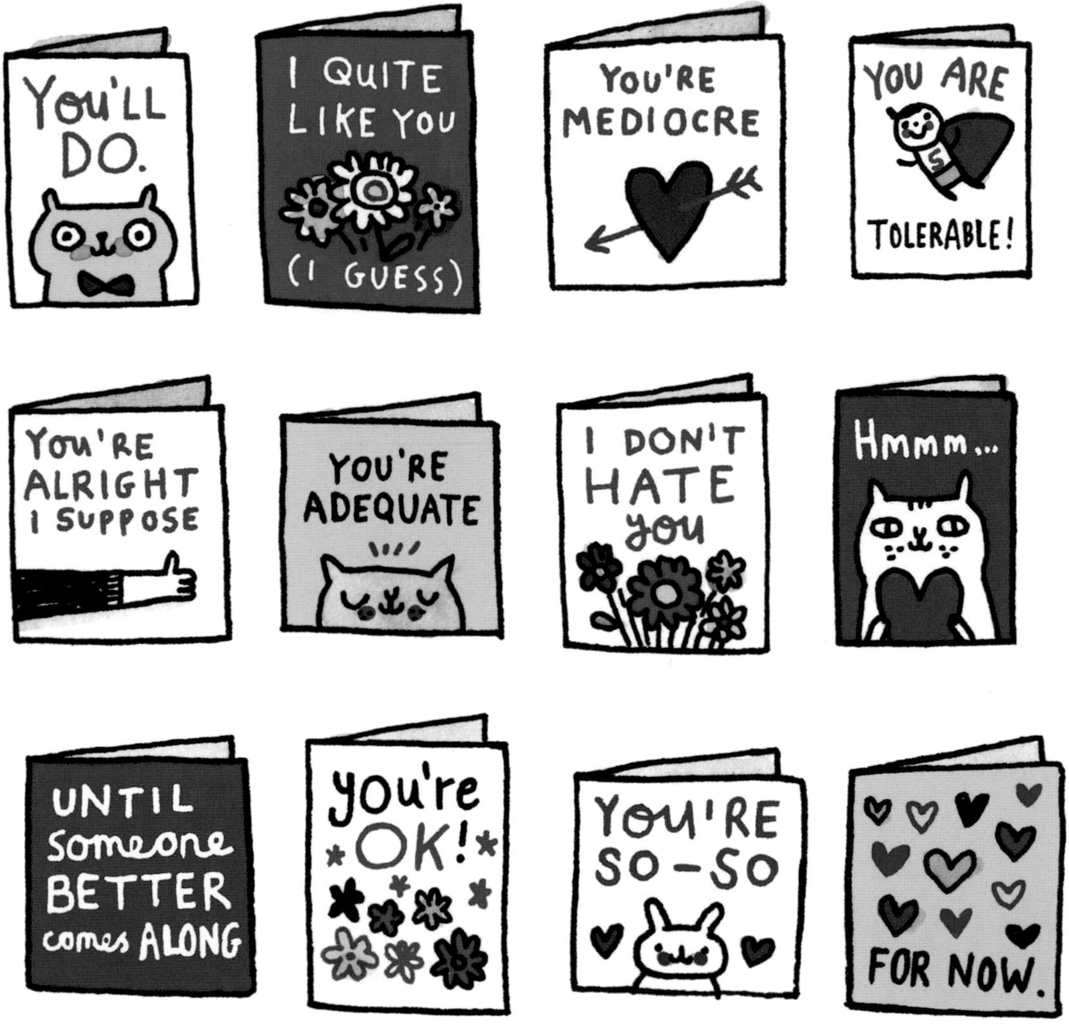

YOU'LL DO.
I QUITE LIKE YOU (I GUESS)
YOU'RE MEDIOCRE
YOU ARE TOLERABLE!
S
YOU'RE ALRIGHT I SUPPOSE
YOU'RE ADEQUATE
I DON'T HATE YOU
Hmmm...
UNTIL Someone BETTER comes ALONG
you're OK!
YOU'RE SO-SO
FOR NOW.

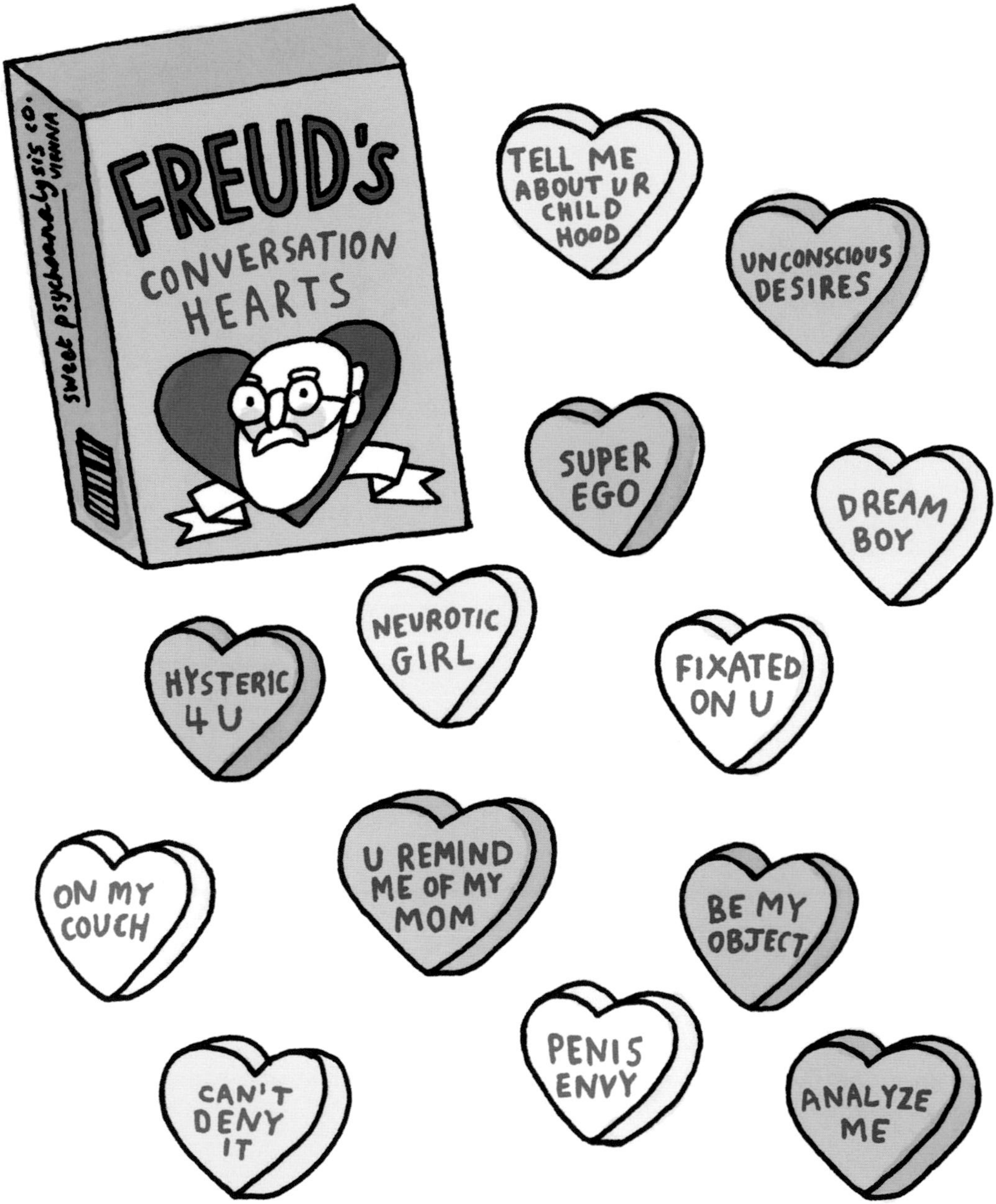
sweet psychoanalysis co.
VIENNA
FREUD's
CONVERSATION HEARTS
TELL ME ABOUT UR CHILD HOOD
UNCONSCIOUS DESIRES
SUPER EGO
DREAM BOY
NEUROTIC GIRL
HYSTERIC 4 U
FIXATED ON U
ON MY COUCH
U REMIND ME OF MY MOM
BE MY OBJECT
PENIS ENVY
CAN'T DENY IT
ANALYZE ME

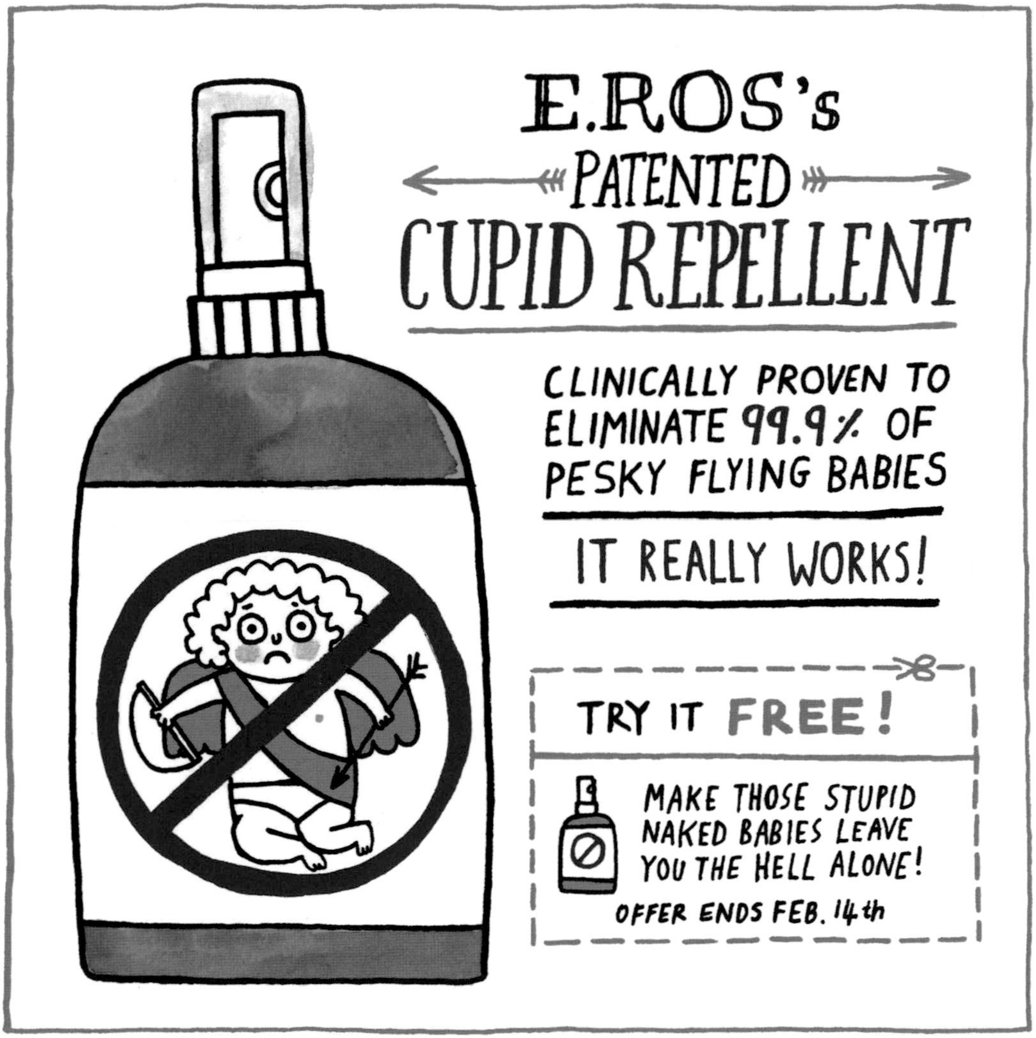
E.ROS's
PATENTED
CUPID REPELLENT
CLINICALLY PROVEN TO ELIMINATE 99.9% OF PESKY FLYING BABIES
IT REALLY WORKS!
TRY IT FREE!
MAKE THOSE STUPID NAKED BABIES LEAVE YOU THE HELL ALONE!
OFFER ENDS FEB. 14th

THE ^UPDATED^ LANGUAGE OF FLOWERS

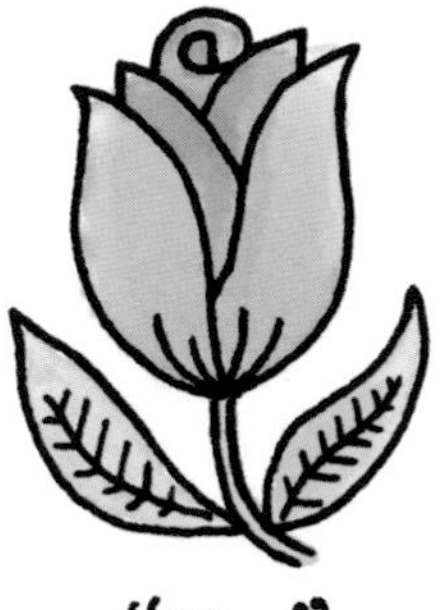

"Yes"

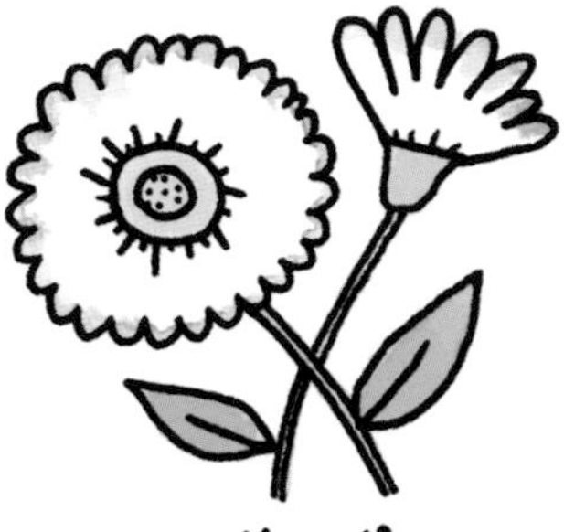

"No"

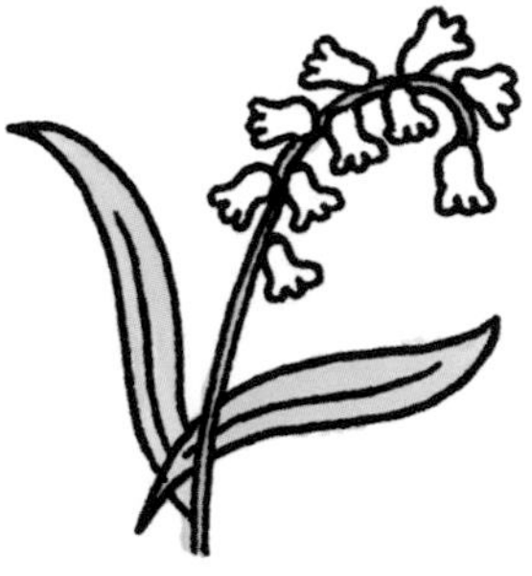

"Whatever"

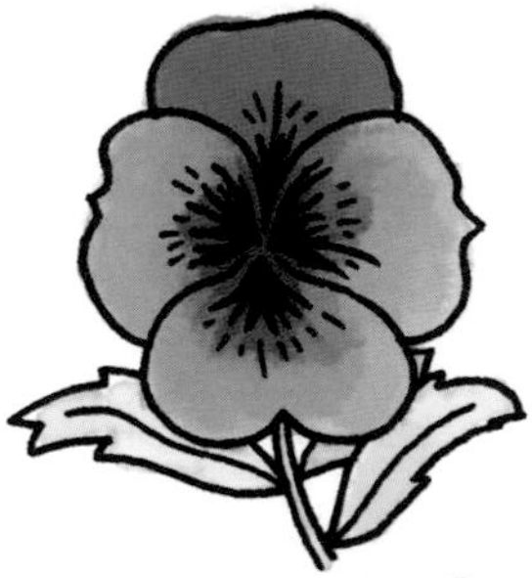

"Your text received"

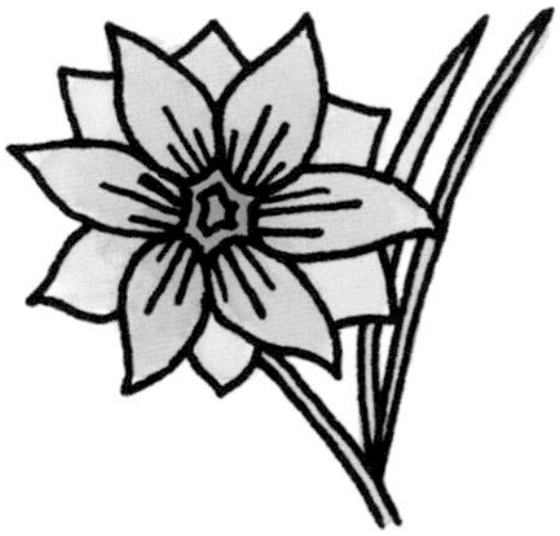

"I await your e-mail"

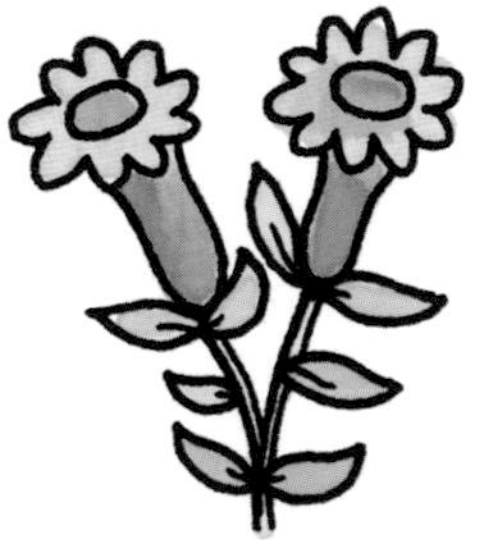

"I regret that I am emotionally unavailable"

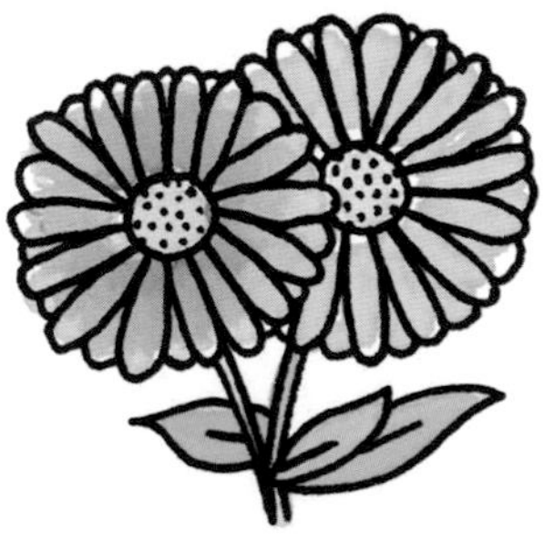

"Your Profile pic charms me"

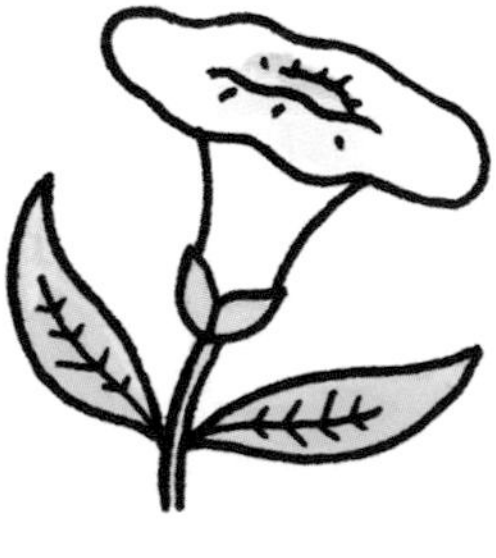

"I love You, but I'm not in love with you"

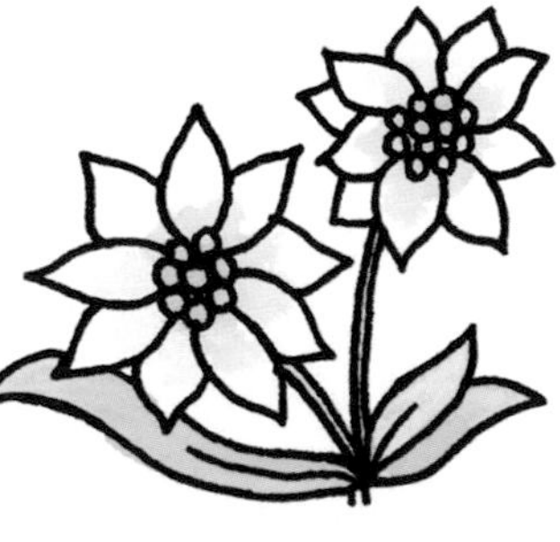

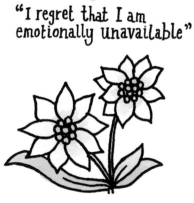

"We are all hurtling towards death"

SVETLANA'S SECRET *Lingerie*

THE GIFT THAT *every* WOMAN WANTS THIS VALENTINE'S DAY!

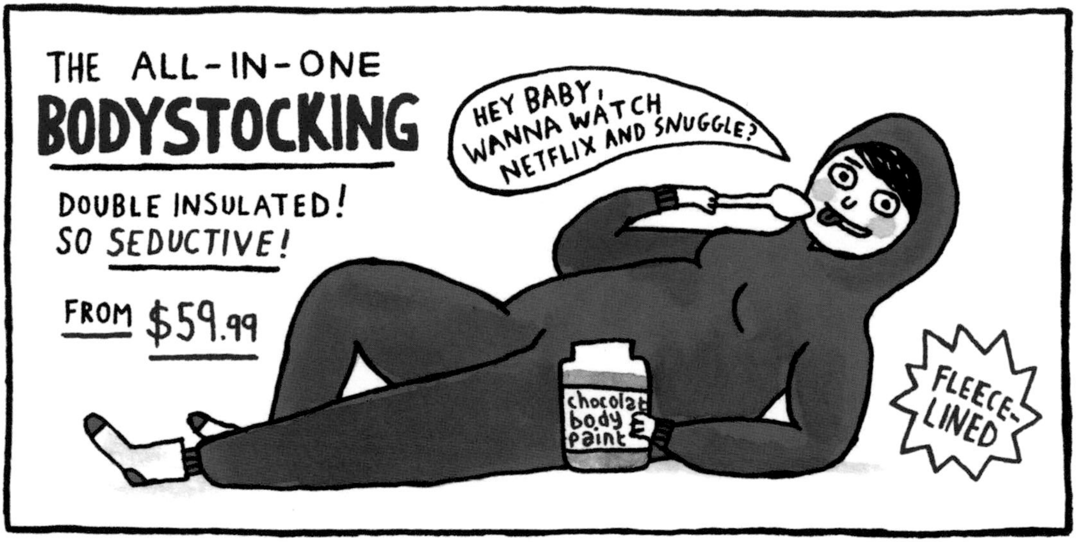
THE ALL-IN-ONE
BODYSTOCKING
DOUBLE INSULATED!
SO SEDUCTIVE!
FROM $59.99
HEY BABY, WANNA WATCH NETFLIX AND SNUGGLE?
chocolate body paint
FLEECE-LINED

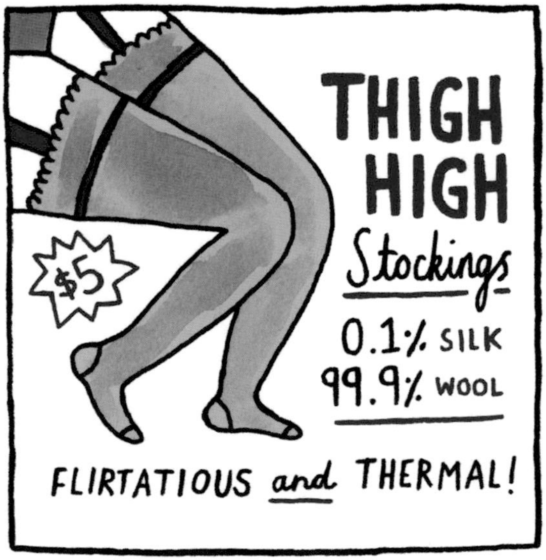
$5
THIGH HIGH
Stockings
0.1% SILK
99.9% WOOL
FLIRTATIOUS and THERMAL!

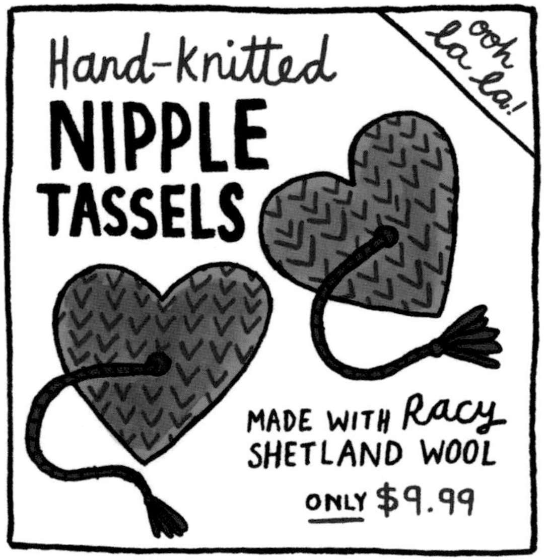
ooh la la!
Hand-knitted
NIPPLE TASSELS
MADE WITH Racy SHETLAND WOOL
ONLY $9.99

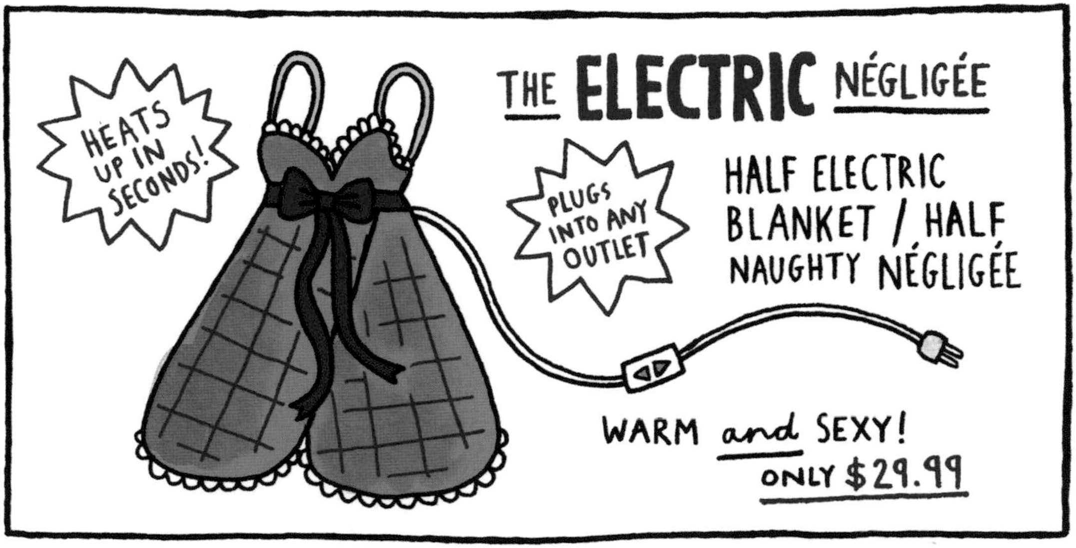
HEATS UP IN SECONDS!
THE ELECTRIC NÉGLIGÉE
PLUGS INTO ANY OUTLET
HALF ELECTRIC BLANKET / HALF NAUGHTY NÉGLIGÉE
WARM and SEXY!
ONLY $29.99

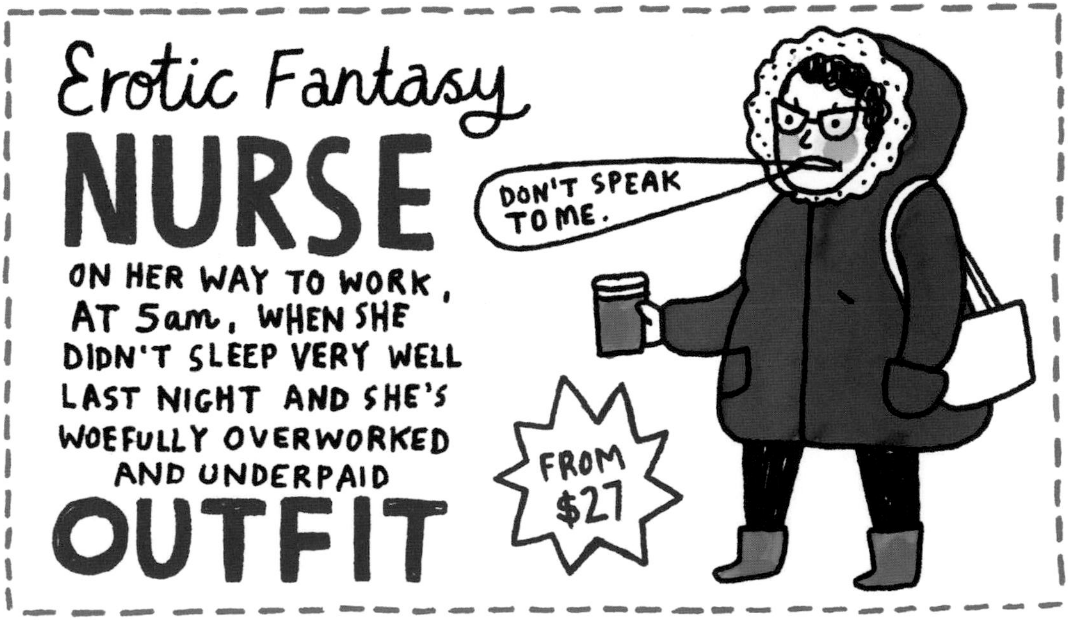
Erotic Fantasy
NURSE
ON HER WAY TO WORK, AT 5am, WHEN SHE DIDN'T SLEEP VERY WELL LAST NIGHT AND SHE'S WOEFULLY OVERWORKED AND UNDERPAID
OUTFIT
DON'T SPEAK TO ME.
FROM $27

A Map of

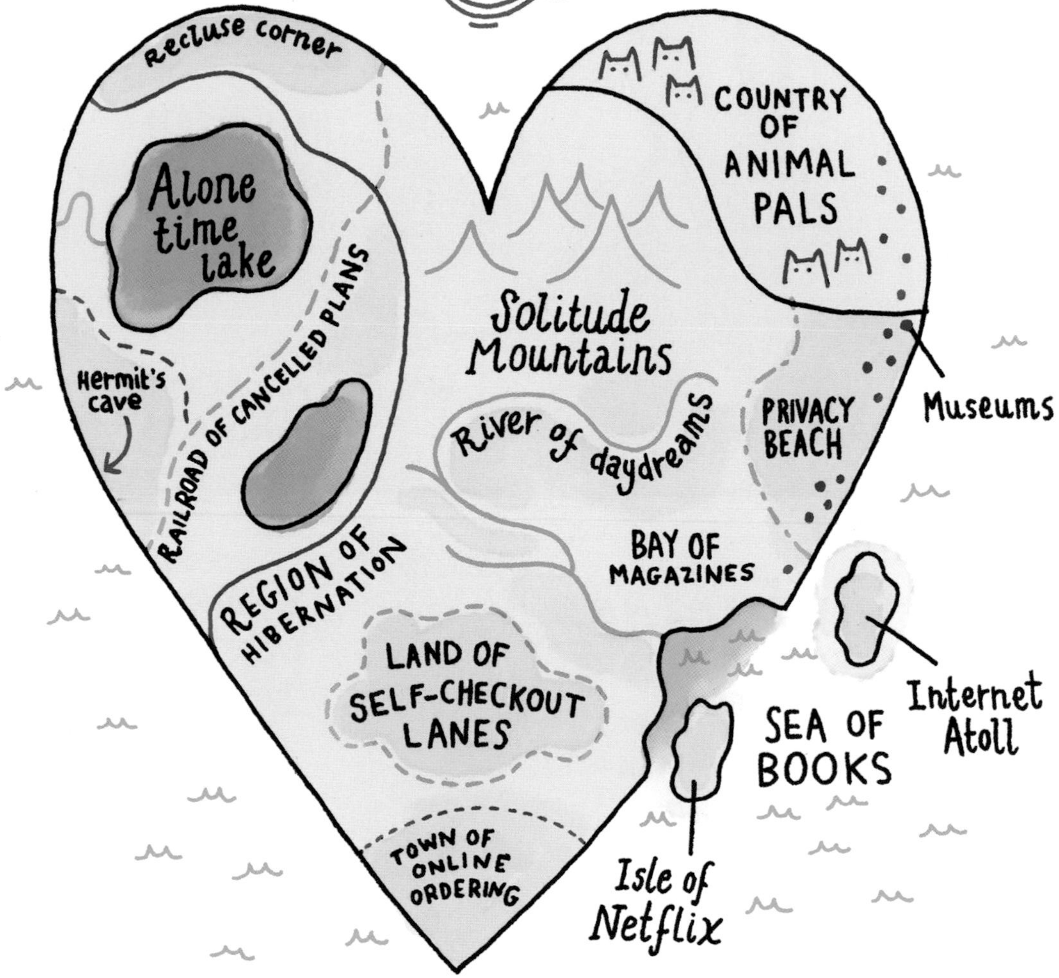
Recluse corner
Alone time lake
Hermit's cave
RAILROAD OF CANCELLED PLANS
REGION OF HIBERNATION
Solitude Mountains
River of daydreams
COUNTRY OF ANIMAL PALS
PRIVACY BEACH
Museums
BAY OF MAGAZINES
LAND OF SELF-CHECKOUT LANES
TOWN OF ONLINE ORDERING
SEA OF BOOKS
Internet Atoll
Isle of Netflix

The Introvert's Heart*

BY AN INTROVERT

*NO CELL PHONE RECEPTION

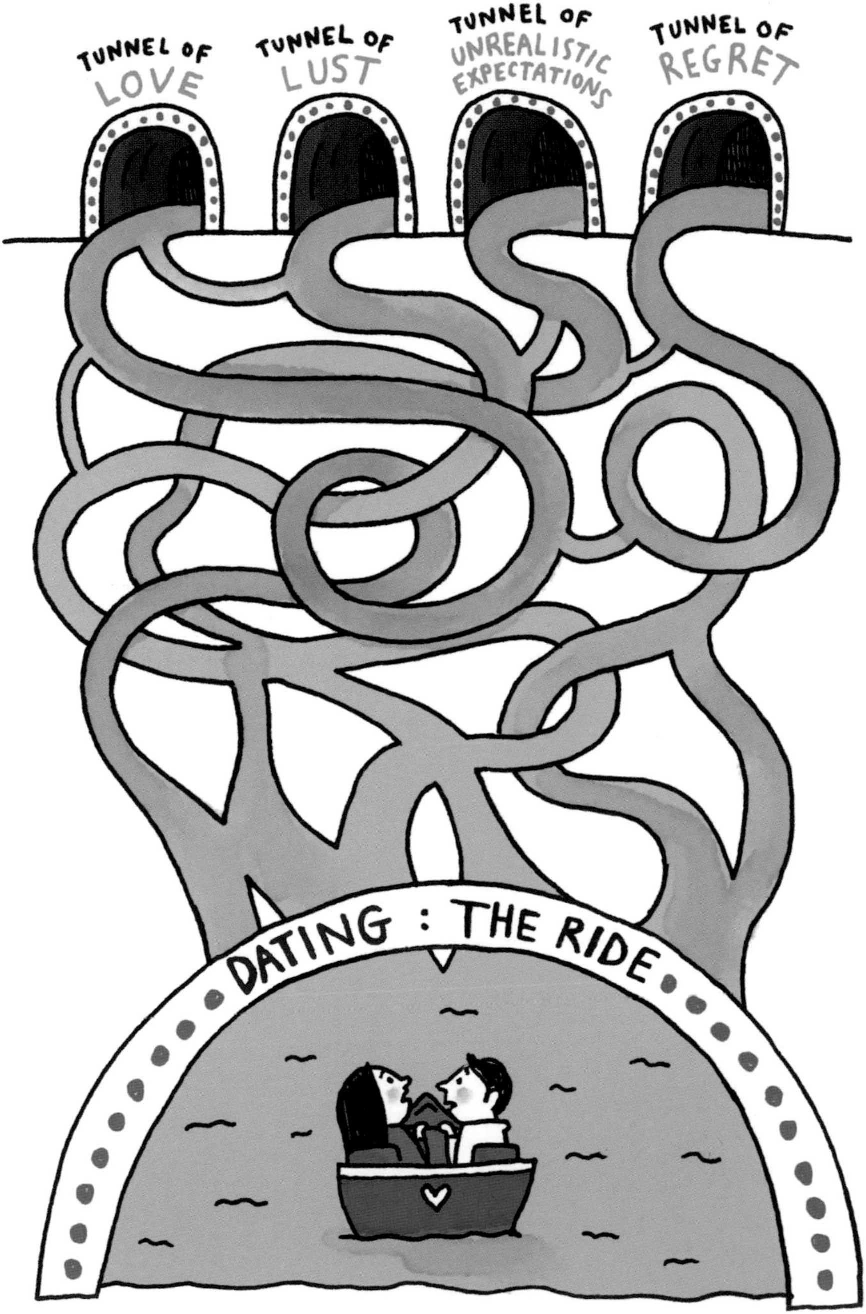
TUNNEL OF
LOVE
TUNNEL OF
LUST
TUNNEL OF
UNREALISTIC EXPECTATIONS
TUNNEL OF
REGRET
DATING : THE RIDE

PARTY DRINKS FOR THE SOCIALLY ANXIOUS

HARVEY WALLFLOWER

Mix Vodka and Orange juice. Add hazelnut liqueur and stir. Enjoy while standing very quietly in a dark corner, hoping that nobody notices you.

A GOOD BOOK ON THE BEACH

Add Vodka, Peach Schnapps, Orange juice, and Cranberry juice to a highball glass.

Sit back and dream of being somewhere — anywhere - but here.

FLAMING HANGOVER

Dump whatever alcohol you can find into a mug. Drink until you feel ready to start flailing your limbs around in a vague approximation of "dancing."

WHERE YOU WILL FIND ME AT PARTIES...

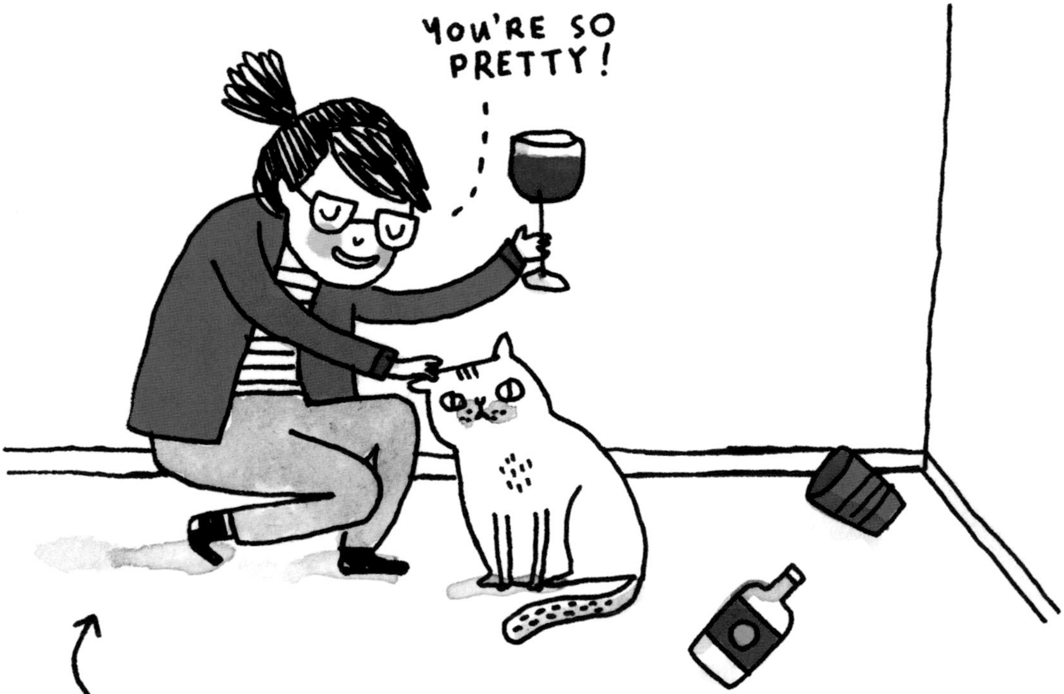
YOU'RE SO PRETTY!

MAKING FRIENDS WITH THE RESIDENT ANIMALS, LIKE A DRUNKEN SNOW WHITE.

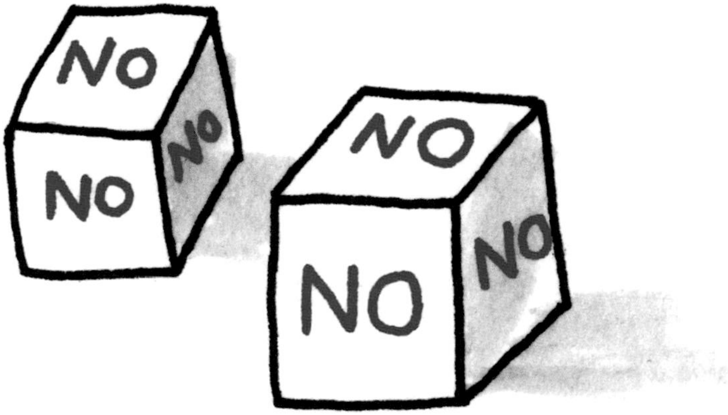
NO
NO
NO
NO
NO
NO

DECISION MAKING DICE
FOR MY SOCIAL LIFE

REAL LIFE HORROR MOVIES

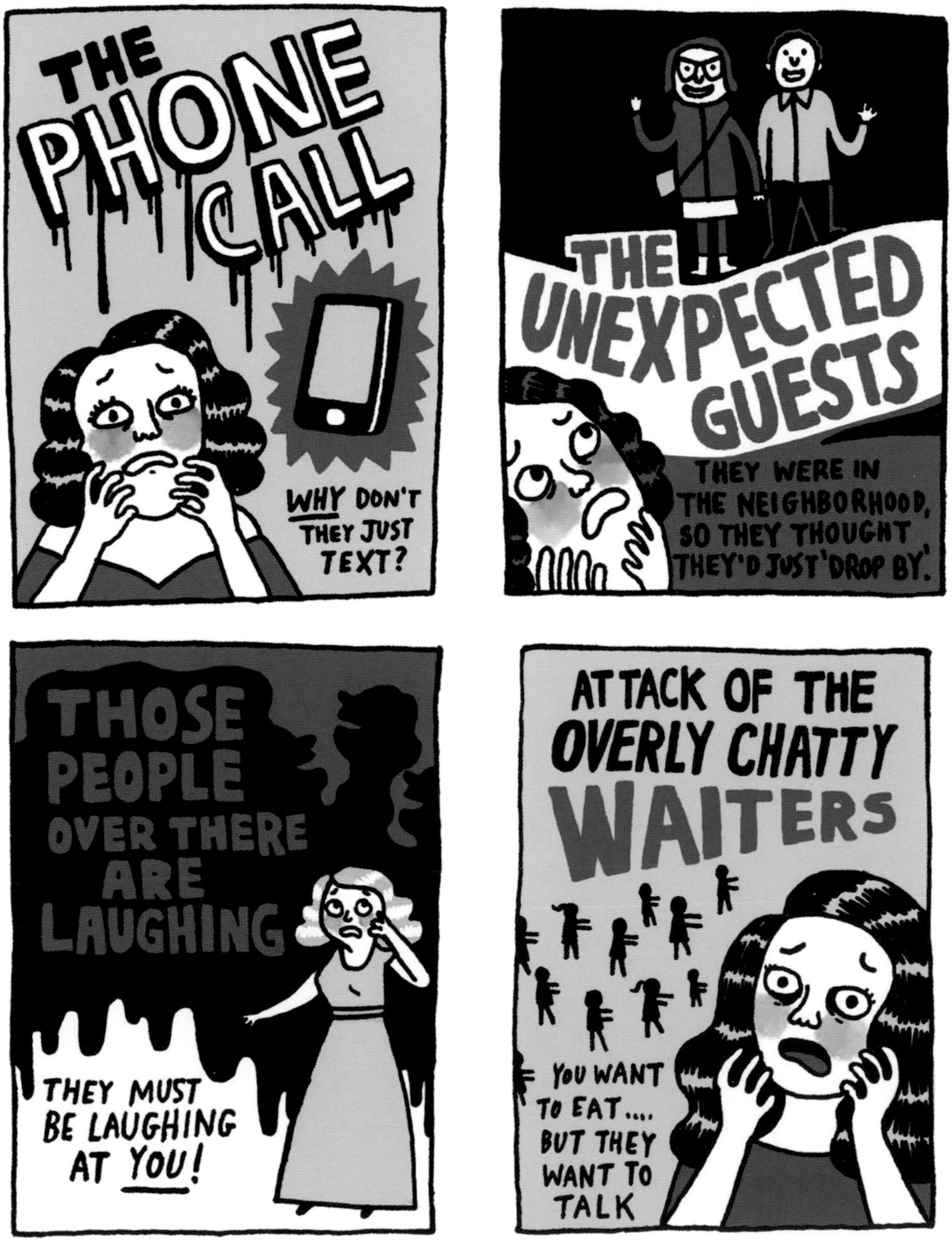
THE PHONE CALL
WHY DON'T THEY JUST TEXT?
THE UNEXPECTED GUESTS
THEY WERE IN THE NEIGHBORHOOD, SO THEY THOUGHT THEY'D JUST 'DROP BY'.
THOSE PEOPLE OVER THERE ARE LAUGHING
THEY MUST BE LAUGHING AT YOU!
ATTACK OF THE OVERLY CHATTY WAITERS
YOU WANT TO EAT.... BUT THEY WANT TO TALK

CHAPTER FIVE

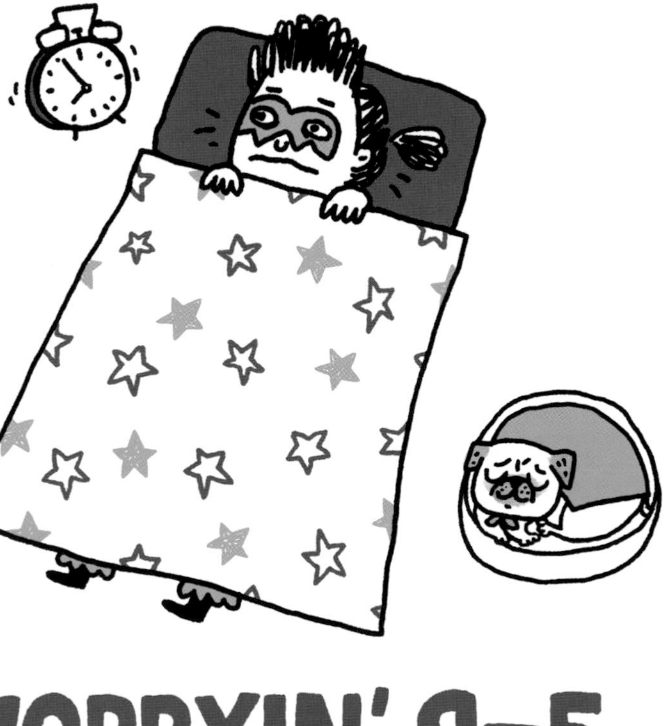

WORRYIN' 9–5

ANGST FOR GROWN-UPS

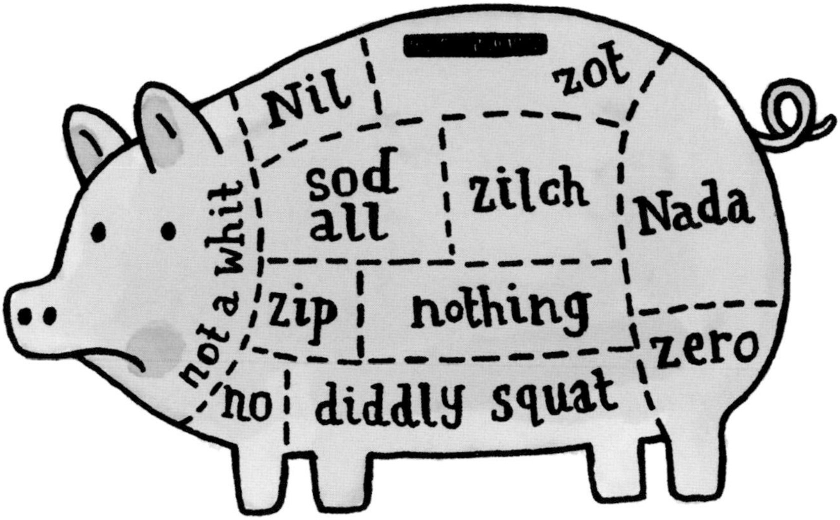
Nil
zot
sod all
zilch
Nada
not a whit
zip
nothing
zero
no
diddly squat

MY SAVINGS ACCOUNT : PRIME CUTS

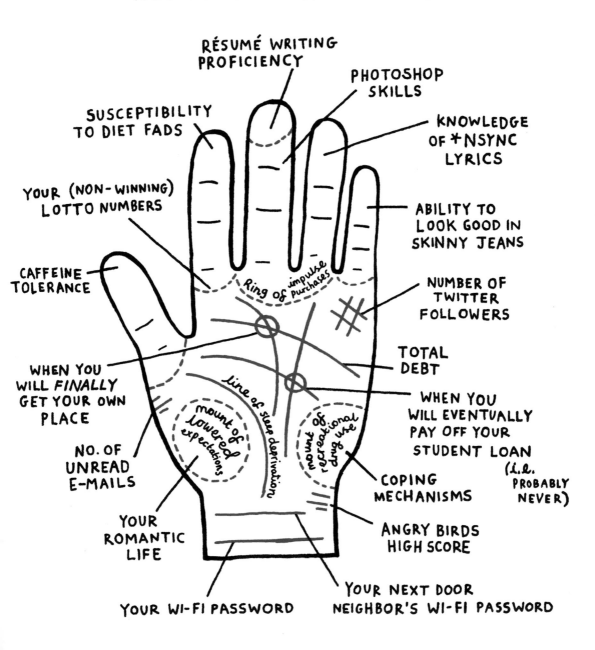

PALM READING FOR MILLENNIALS

RÉSUMÉ WRITING PROFICIENCY

PHOTOSHOP SKILLS

SUSCEPTIBILITY TO DIET FADS

KNOWLEDGE OF *NSYNC LYRICS

YOUR (NON-WINNING) LOTTO NUMBERS

ABILITY TO LOOK GOOD IN SKINNY JEANS

CAFFEINE TOLERANCE

Ring of impulse purchases

NUMBER OF TWITTER FOLLOWERS

TOTAL DEBT

WHEN YOU WILL FINALLY GET YOUR OWN PLACE

line of sleep deprivation

mount of lowered expectations

mount of recreational drug use

WHEN YOU WILL EVENTUALLY PAY OFF YOUR STUDENT LOAN

(i.e. PROBABLY NEVER)

NO. OF UNREAD E-MAILS

COPING MECHANISMS

YOUR ROMANTIC LIFE

ANGRY BIRDS HIGH SCORE

YOUR WI-FI PASSWORD

YOUR NEXT DOOR NEIGHBOR'S WI-FI PASSWORD

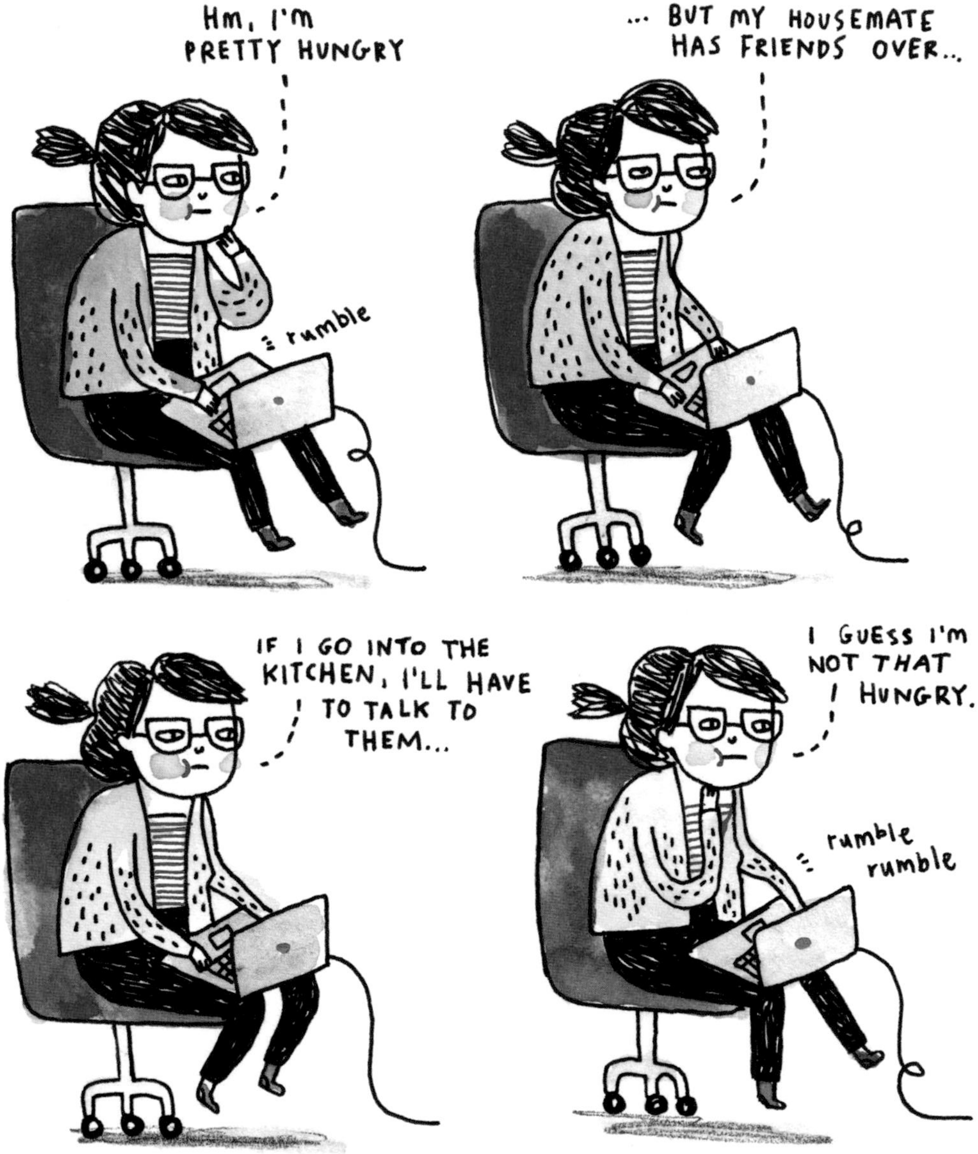
HM, I'M PRETTY HUNGRY
rumble
... BUT MY HOUSEMATE HAS FRIENDS OVER...
IF I GO INTO THE KITCHEN, I'LL HAVE TO TALK TO THEM...
I GUESS I'M NOT *THAT* HUNGRY.
rumble rumble

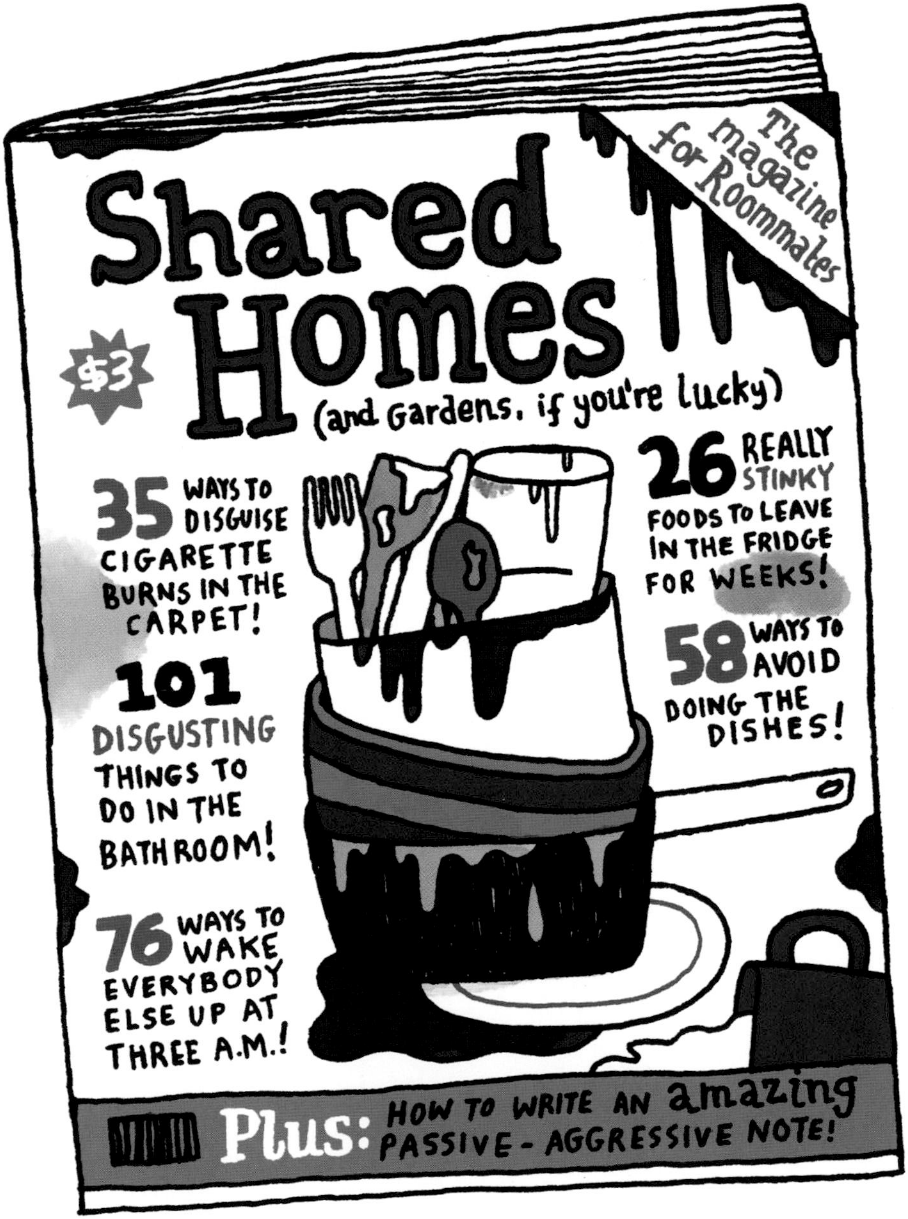

The magazine for Roommates
Shared Homes
$3
(and Gardens, if you're lucky)
35 WAYS TO DISGUISE CIGARETTE BURNS IN THE CARPET!
101 DISGUSTING THINGS TO DO IN THE BATHROOM!
76 WAYS TO WAKE EVERYBODY ELSE UP AT THREE A.M.!
26 REALLY STINKY FOODS TO LEAVE IN THE FRIDGE FOR WEEKS!
58 WAYS TO AVOID DOING THE DISHES!
Plus: HOW TO WRITE AN amazing PASSIVE-AGGRESSIVE NOTE!

URBAN AROMAS

FRAGRANCES INSPIRED BY THE DAILY COMMUTE

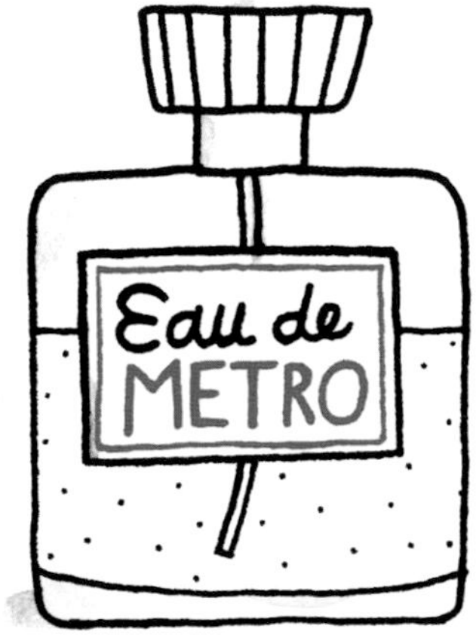
Eau de
METRO

HIGHLY CARCINOGENIC, WITH NOTES OF MORNING BREATH AND WET CONCRETE.

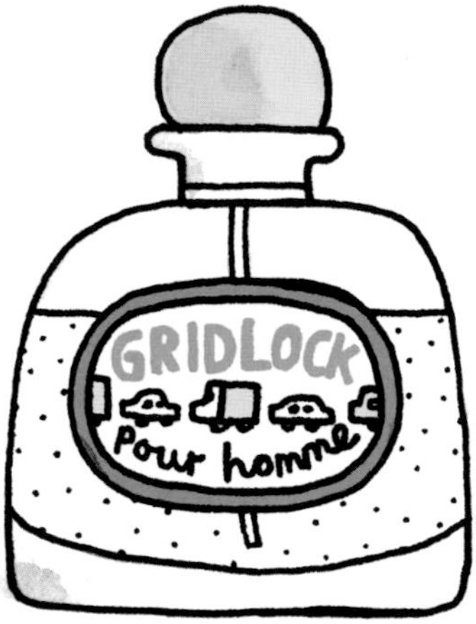
GRIDLOCK
Pour homme

REMINISCENT OF YESTERDAY'S SANDWICHES, WITH TOP NOTES OF FEET AND RESENTMENT.

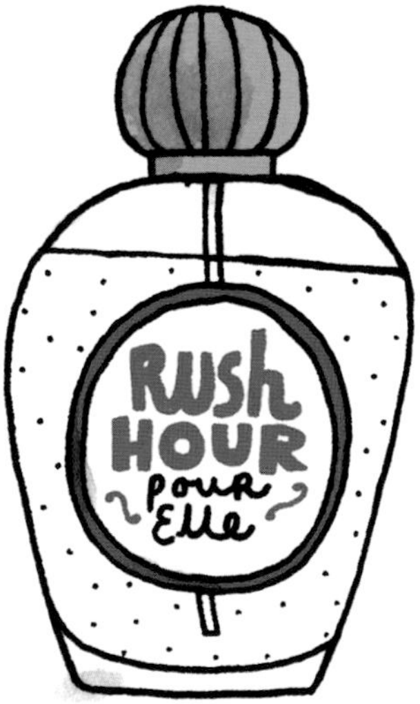
RUSH
HOUR
pour
Elle

BRINGS TO MIND THAT NAGGING FEELING THAT THERE MUST BE MORE TO LIFE THAN THIS.

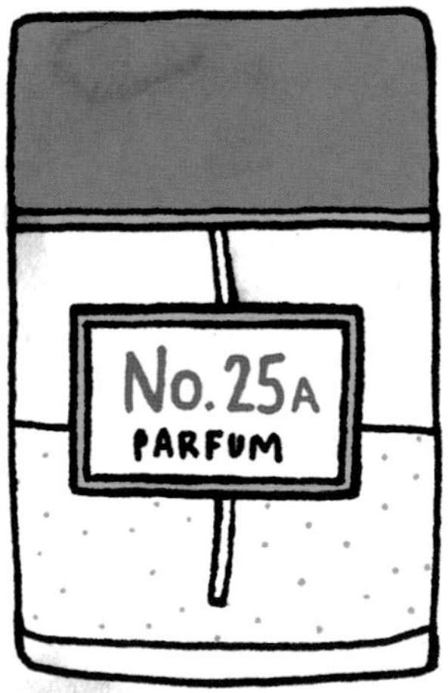
No. 25A
PARFUM

A HEADY BLEND OF UNWASHED BODIES, GASOLINE, AND MISERY.

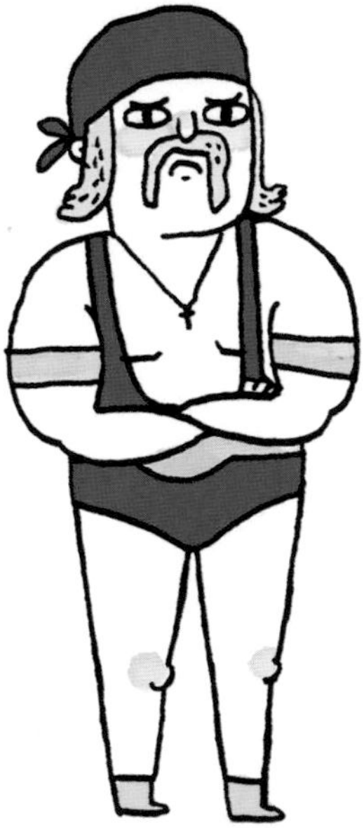

SULK HOGAN

SIGNATURE MOVE: THE GRUMP

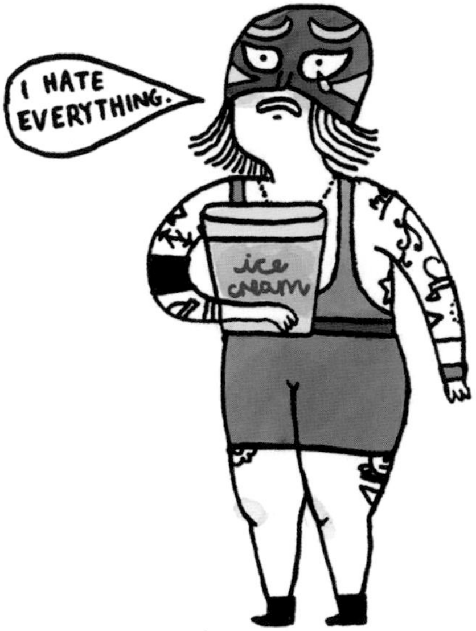
I HATE EVERYTHING.
ice cream

REY PMS-TERIO

SIGNATURE MOVE: THE MOOD SWING

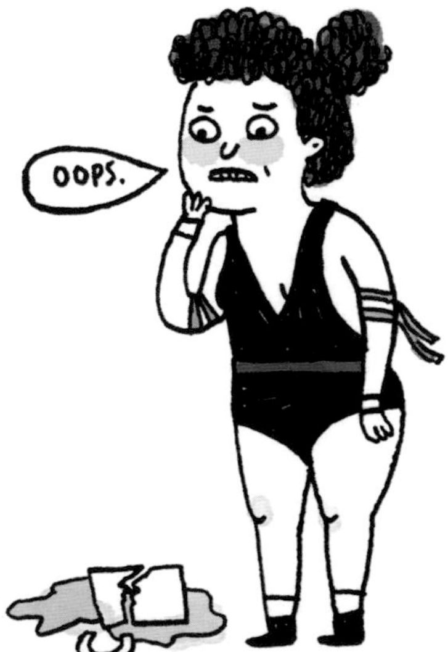
OOPS.

ANDREA, THE GIANT KLUTZ

SIGNATURE MOVE:
THE FACEPLANT

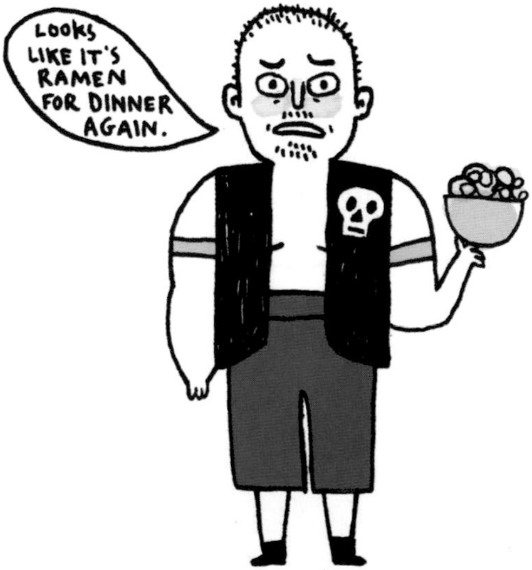
LOOKS LIKE IT'S RAMEN FOR DINNER AGAIN.

STONE BROKE STEVE AUSTIN

SIGNATURE MOVE:
THE BOUNCING RENT CHECK

I WISH I STILL GOT STICKERS FOR DOING HARD STUFF.

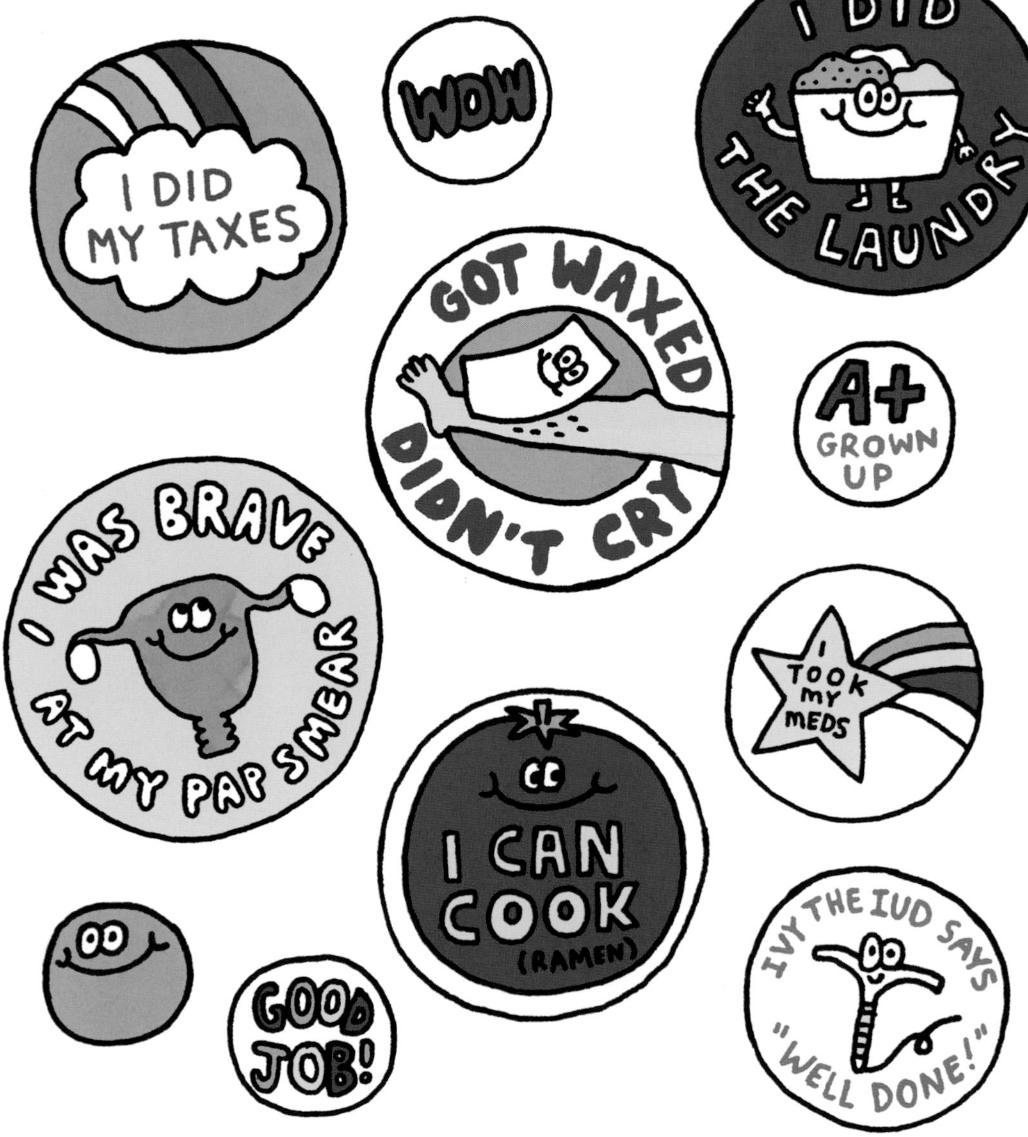
I DID MY TAXES
WOW
I DID THE LAUNDRY
GOT WAXED DIDN'T CRY
A+ GROWN UP
I WAS BRAVE AT MY PAP SMEAR
I TOOK MY MEDS
I CAN COOK (RAMEN)
GOOD JOB!
IVY THE IUD SAYS "WELL DONE!"

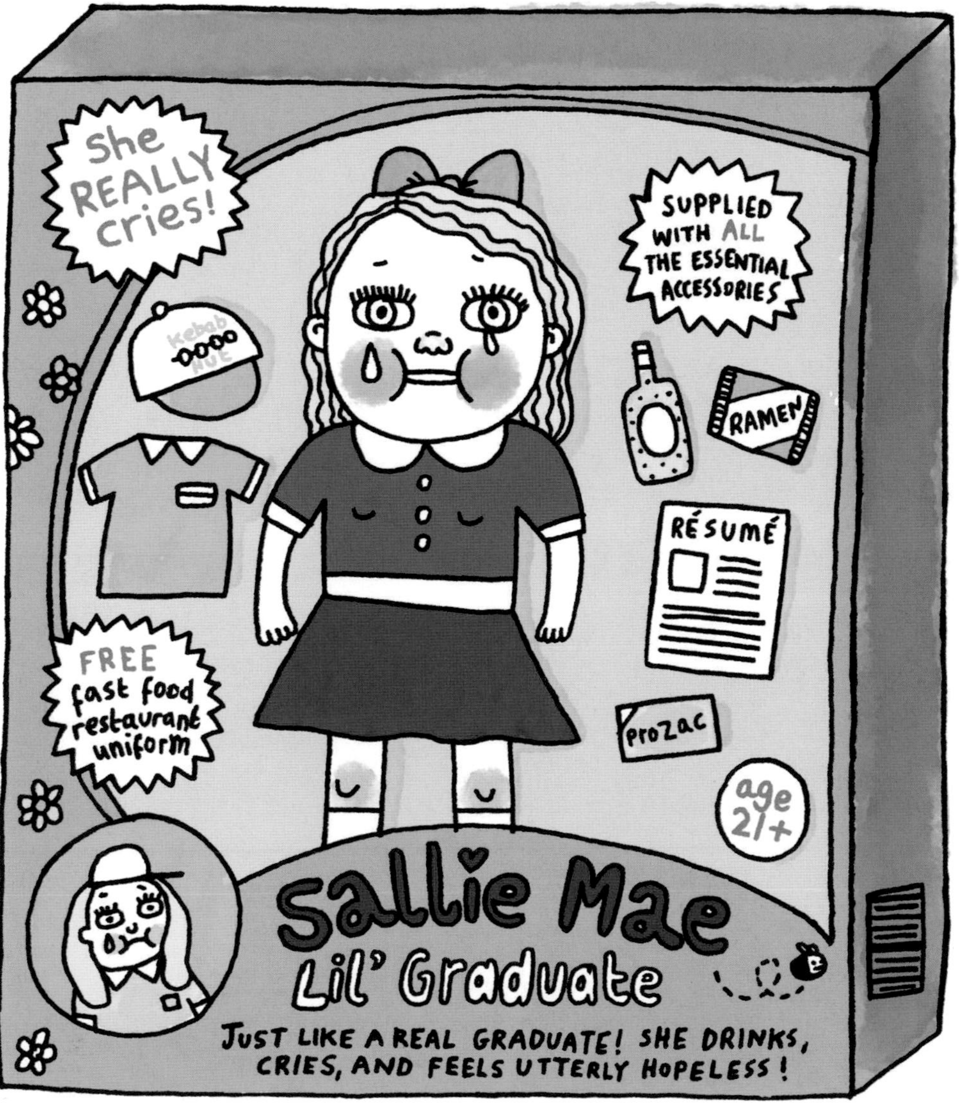
She REALLY cries!
SUPPLIED WITH ALL THE ESSENTIAL ACCESSORIES
Kebab Hut
RAMEN
RÉSUMÉ
FREE fast food restaurant uniform
prozac
age 21+
Sallie Mae
Lil' Graduate
JUST LIKE A REAL GRADUATE! SHE DRINKS, CRIES, AND FEELS UTTERLY HOPELESS!

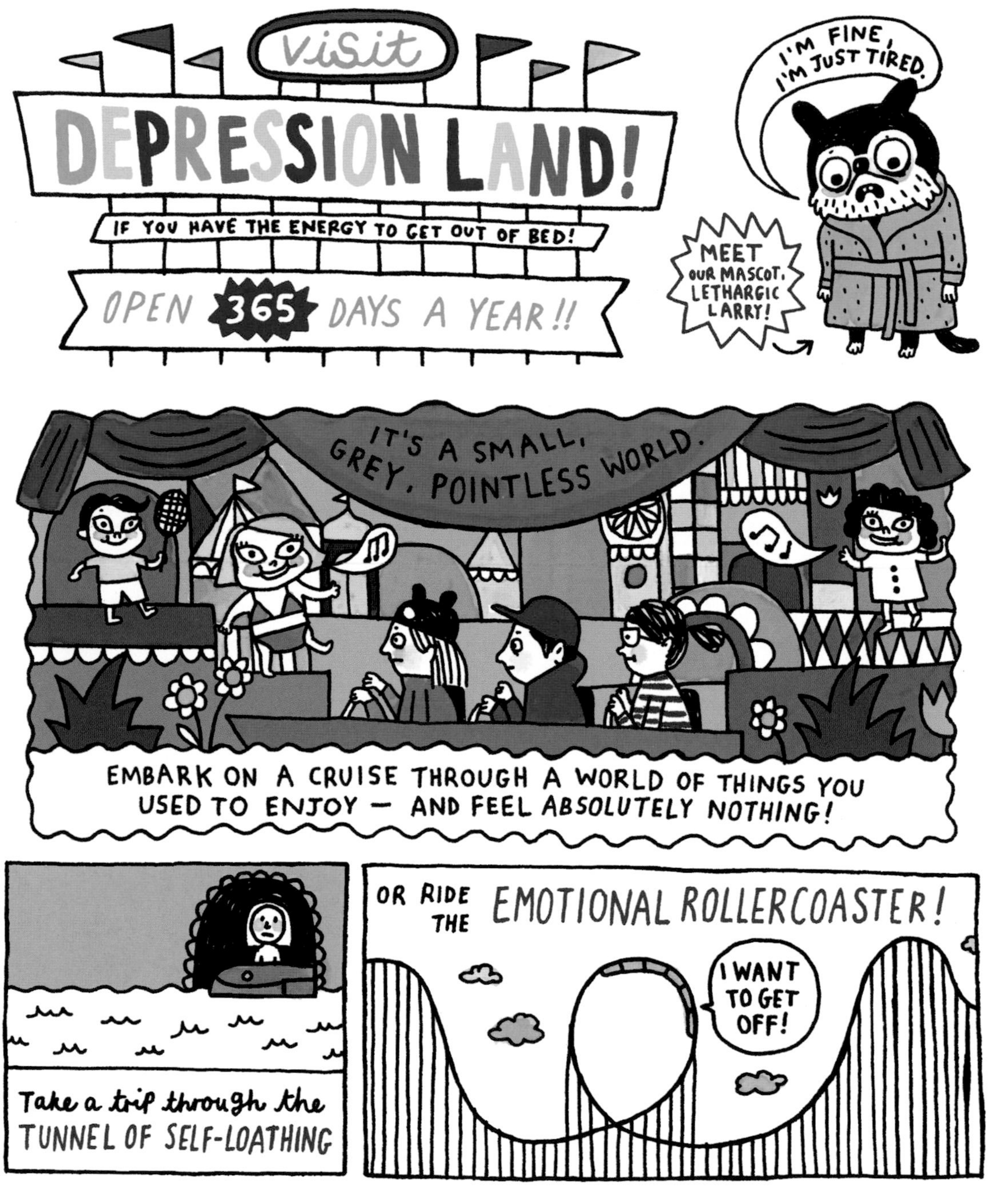

VISIT
DEPRESSION LAND!
IF YOU HAVE THE ENERGY TO GET OUT OF BED!
OPEN 365 DAYS A YEAR!!
I'M FINE, I'M JUST TIRED.
MEET OUR MASCOT, LETHARGIC LARRY!
IT'S A SMALL, GREY, POINTLESS WORLD.
EMBARK ON A CRUISE THROUGH A WORLD OF THINGS YOU USED TO ENJOY — AND FEEL ABSOLUTELY NOTHING!
Take a trip through the TUNNEL OF SELF-LOATHING
OR RIDE THE EMOTIONAL ROLLERCOASTER!
I WANT TO GET OFF!

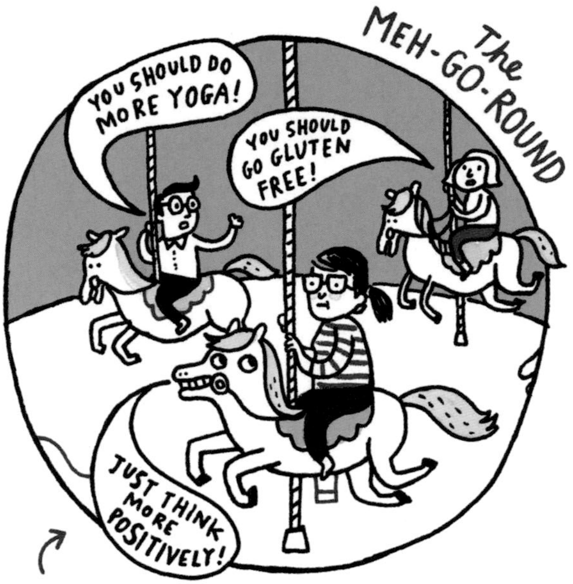
The MEH-GO-ROUND
YOU SHOULD DO MORE YOGA!
YOU SHOULD GO GLUTEN FREE!
JUST THINK MORE POSITIVELY!

HOLD ON TIGHT AS WELL-MEANING FOLK SUGGEST WAYS IN WHICH YOU COULD MAKE YOURSELF BETTER, IF ONLY YOU'D MAKE AN *EFFORT*!

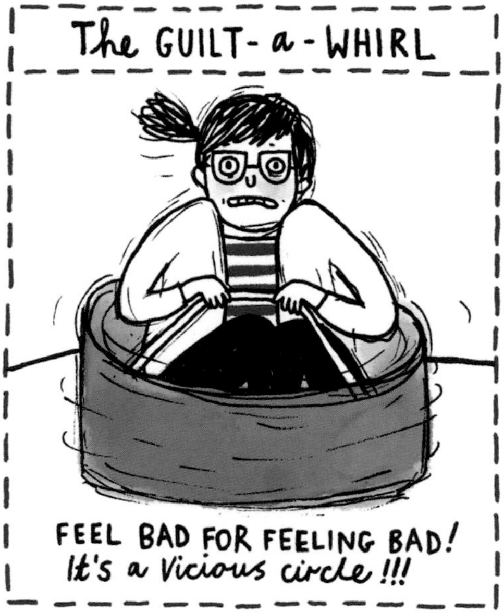
The GUILT-a-WHIRL
FEEL BAD FOR FEELING BAD!
It's a Vicious circle!!!

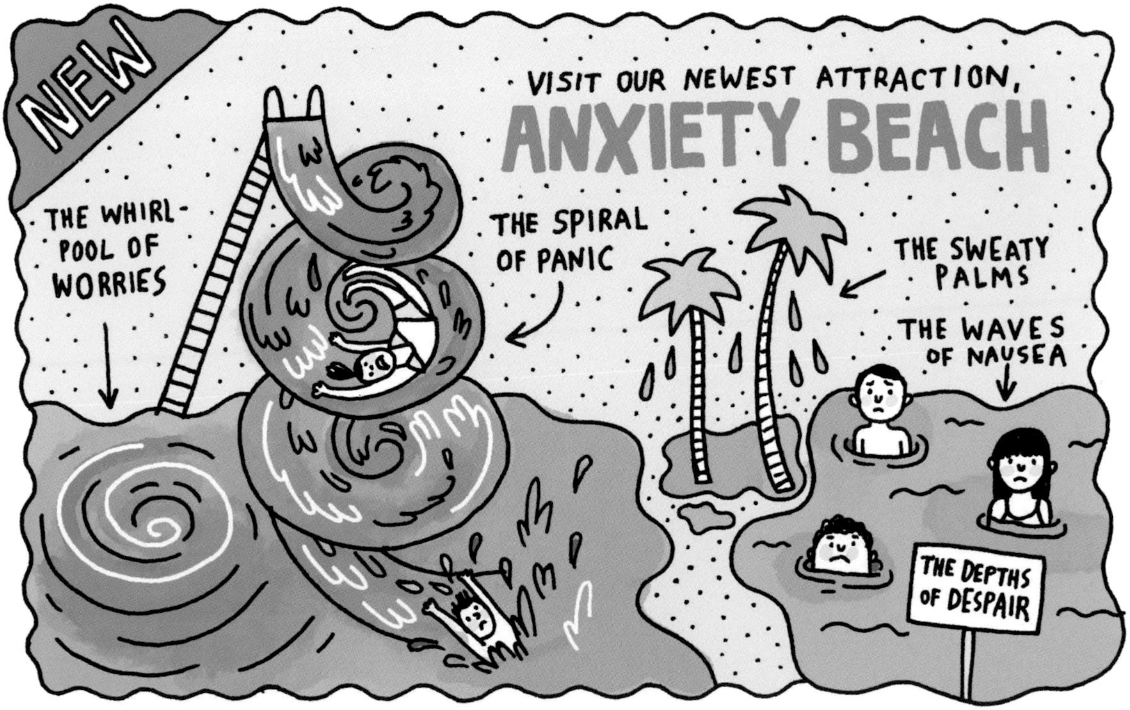
NEW
VISIT OUR NEWEST ATTRACTION,
ANXIETY BEACH
THE WHIRL-POOL OF WORRIES
THE SPIRAL OF PANIC
THE SWEATY PALMS
THE WAVES OF NAUSEA
THE DEPTHS OF DESPAIR

★★★ CHAPTER SIX ★★★

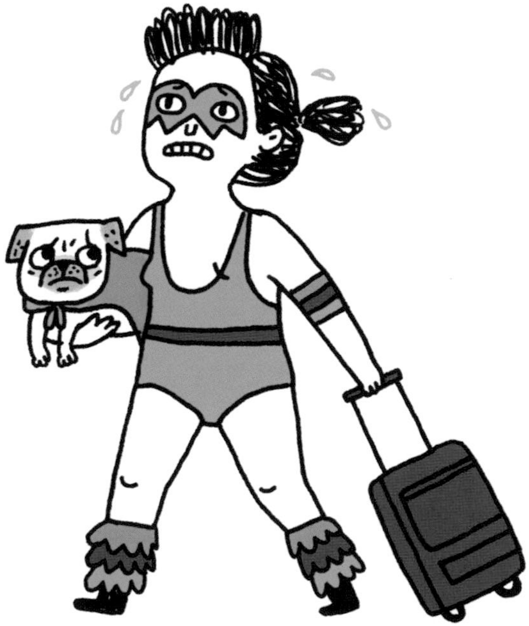

TRAVELS & TRIBULATIONS

ADVERTISEMENT FEATURE

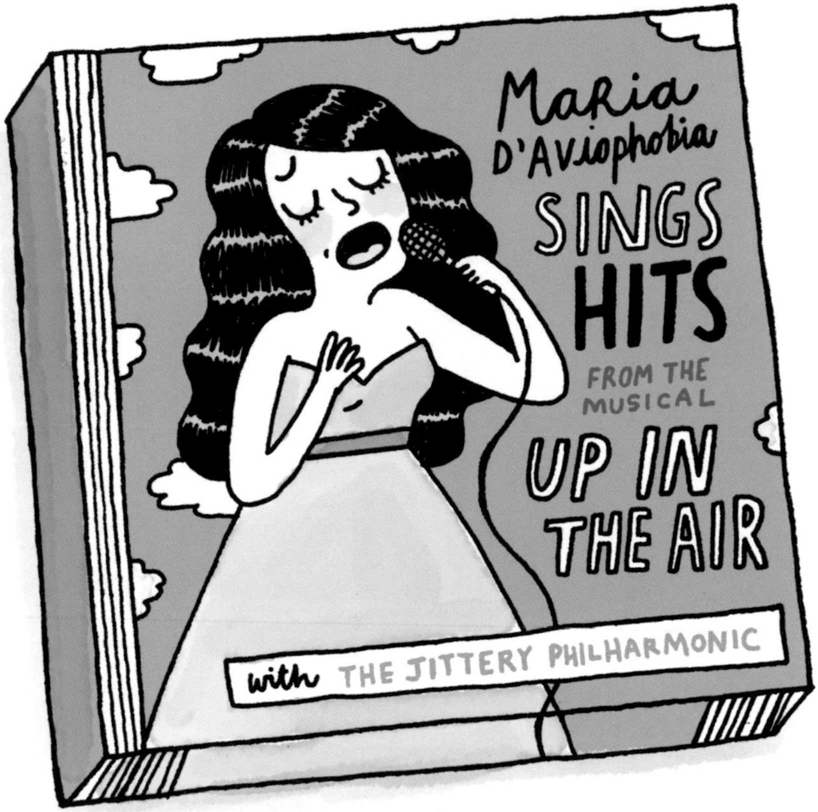
Maria D'Aviophobia
SINGS HITS
FROM THE MUSICAL
UP IN THE AIR
with THE JITTERY PHILHARMONIC

TRACKS INCLUDE:

• WHAT WAS THAT NOISE? • IS THAT NORMAL? •
• BALLAD OF THE SWEATY PALMS • GIVE ME VALIUM •
• THE PANICKING SONG • WHITE KNUCKLES •
• 35,000 FT IN THE AIR (THAT'S 35,000 FT TOO MANY) •
• ARGH! • WHAT WAS THAT NOISE? (REPRISE) •

BUY NOW AND RECEIVE A PAPER BAG TO BREATHE INTO ABSOLUTELY FREE!

MOTELS FOR THE BUDGET-CONSCIOUS TRAVELER

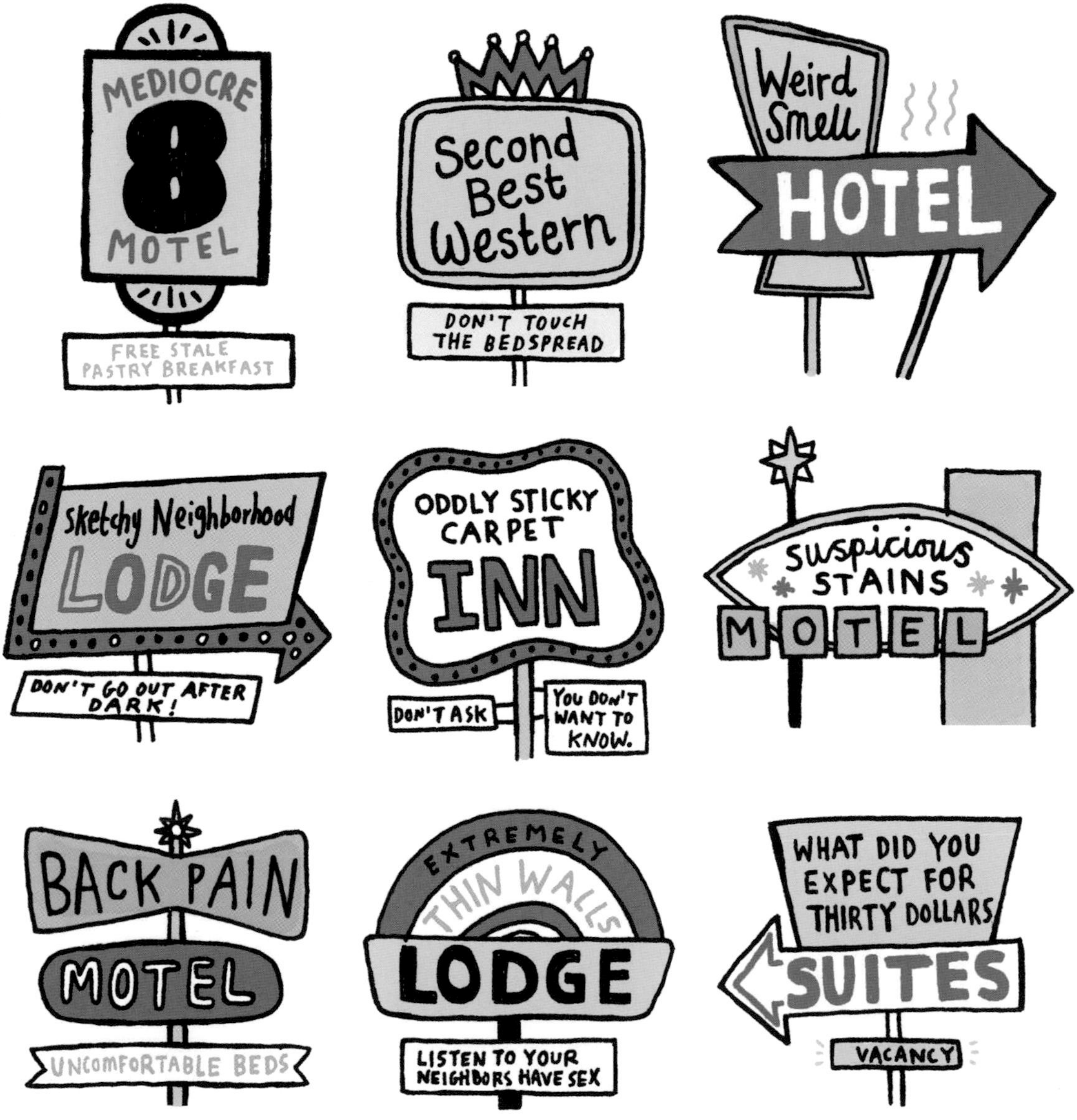
MEDIOCRE
8
MOTEL
FREE STALE PASTRY BREAKFAST
Second Best Western
DON'T TOUCH THE BEDSPREAD
Weird Smell
HOTEL
Sketchy Neighborhood
LODGE
DON'T GO OUT AFTER DARK!
ODDLY STICKY CARPET
INN
DON'T ASK
YOU DON'T WANT TO KNOW.
Suspicious
STAINS
MOTEL
BACK PAIN
MOTEL
UNCOMFORTABLE BEDS
EXTREMELY
THIN WALLS
LODGE
LISTEN TO YOUR NEIGHBORS HAVE SEX
WHAT DID YOU EXPECT FOR THIRTY DOLLARS
SUITES
VACANCY

KNOW YOUR BEACH HAZARD WARNING FLAGS

STRONG CURRENTS

WATERCRAFT

MARINE PESTS

HUMAN PESTS

TRIP HAZARDS

LOW-FLYING
BEACHBALLS

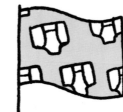

FREE-FLOATING
DIAPERS

GRATUITOUS
MANKINIS

DIRTY THIEVIN'
SEAGULLS

QUESTIONABLE
FAST FOOD

MAN-EATING
LAWNCHAIRS

HYPERACTIVE
TODDLERS

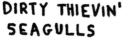

RARE AND COLLECTIBLE SEASHELLS

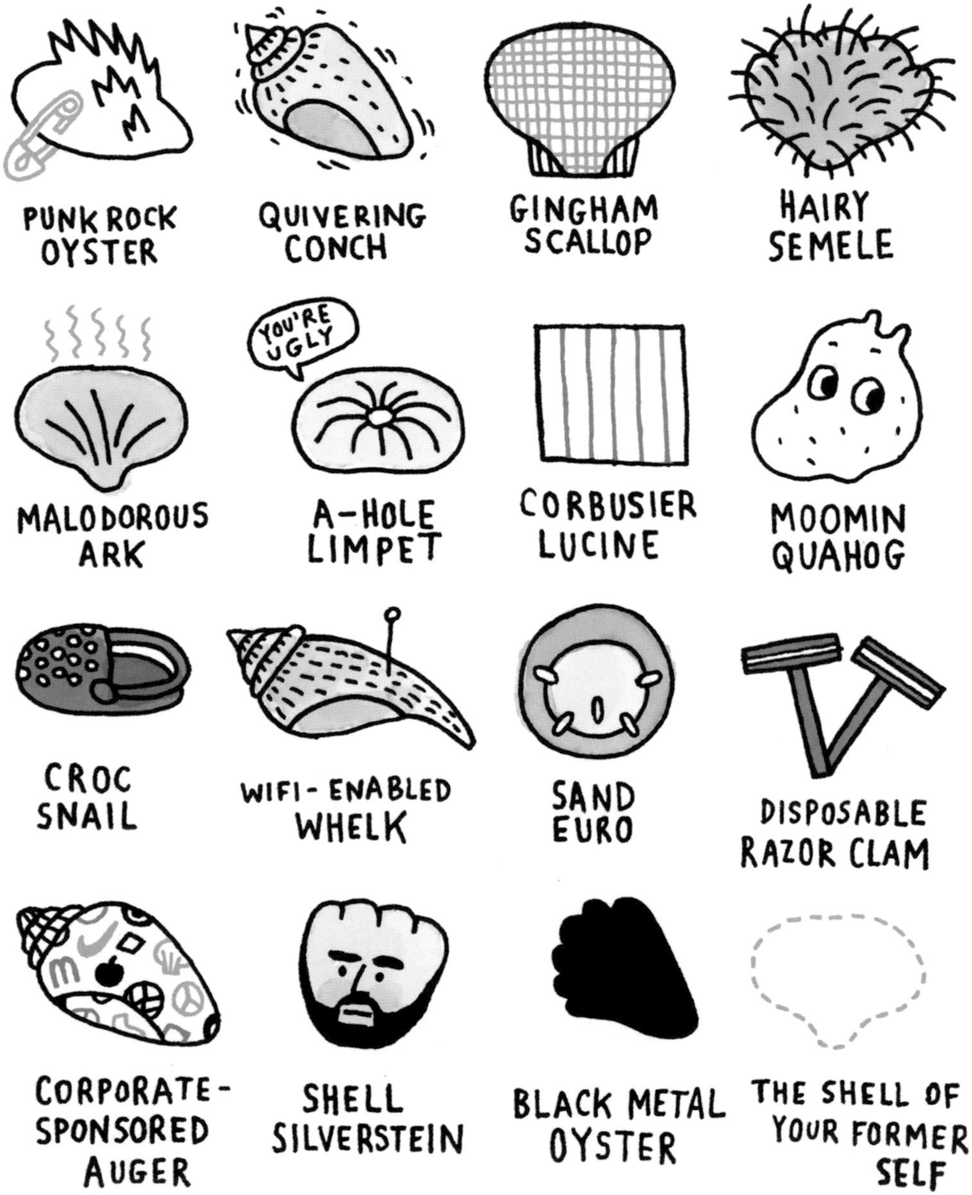
PUNK ROCK OYSTER
QUIVERING CONCH
GINGHAM SCALLOP
HAIRY SEMELE
MALODOROUS ARK
YOU'RE UGLY
A-HOLE LIMPET
CORBUSIER LUCINE
MOOMIN QUAHOG
CROC SNAIL
WIFI-ENABLED WHELK
SAND EURO
DISPOSABLE RAZOR CLAM
CORPORATE-SPONSORED AUGER
SHELL SILVERSTEIN
BLACK METAL OYSTER
THE SHELL OF YOUR FORMER SELF

NORTH AMERICA'S WORST TOURIST "ATTRACTIONS"

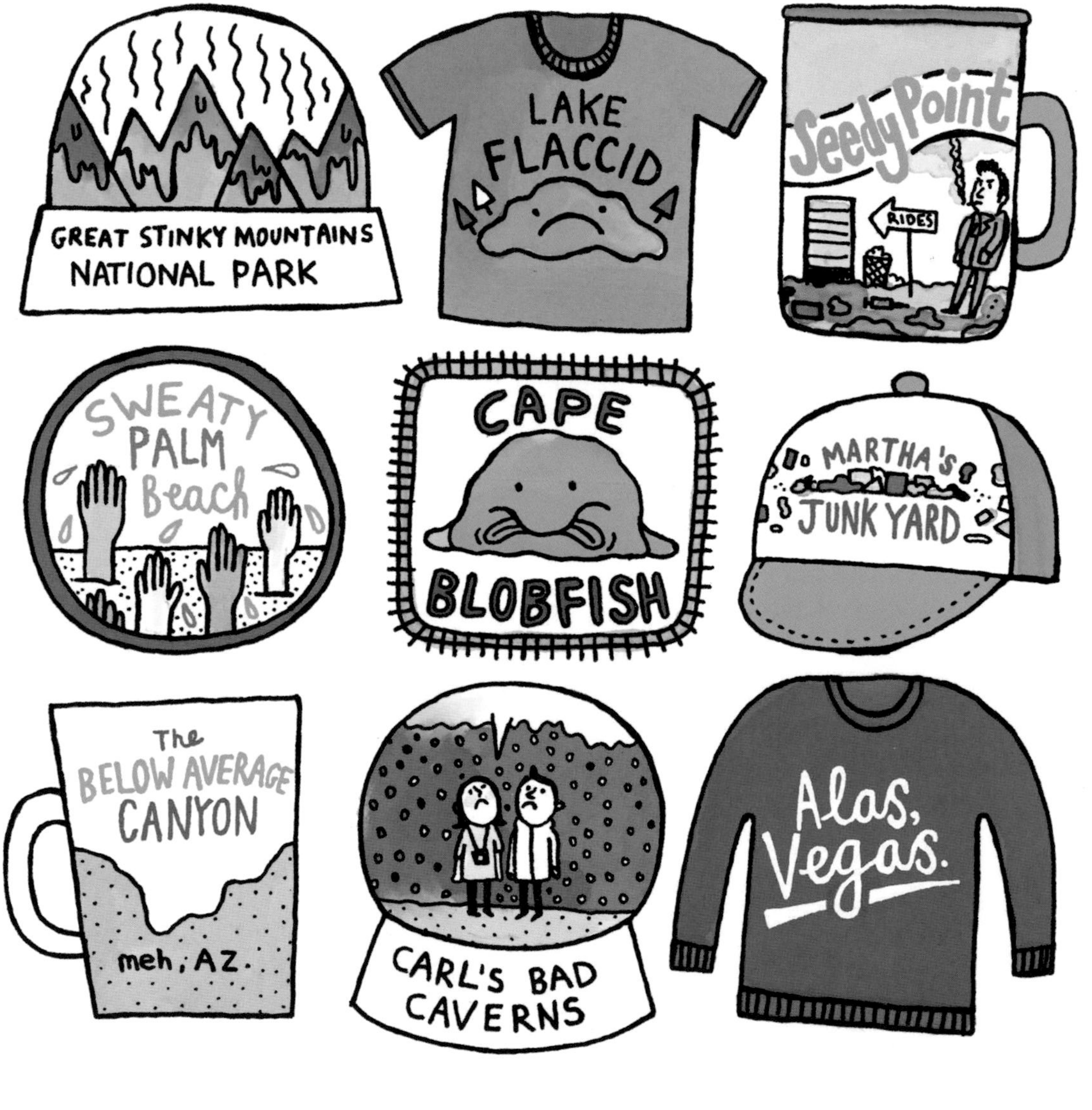
GREAT STINKY MOUNTAINS
NATIONAL PARK
LAKE
FLACCID
Seedy Point
RIDES
SWEATY
PALM
Beach
CAPE
BLOBFISH
MARTHA'S
JUNK YARD
The
BELOW AVERAGE
CANYON
meh, AZ.
CARL'S BAD
CAVERNS
Alas,
Vegas.

MOM'S TRAVEL GUIDES

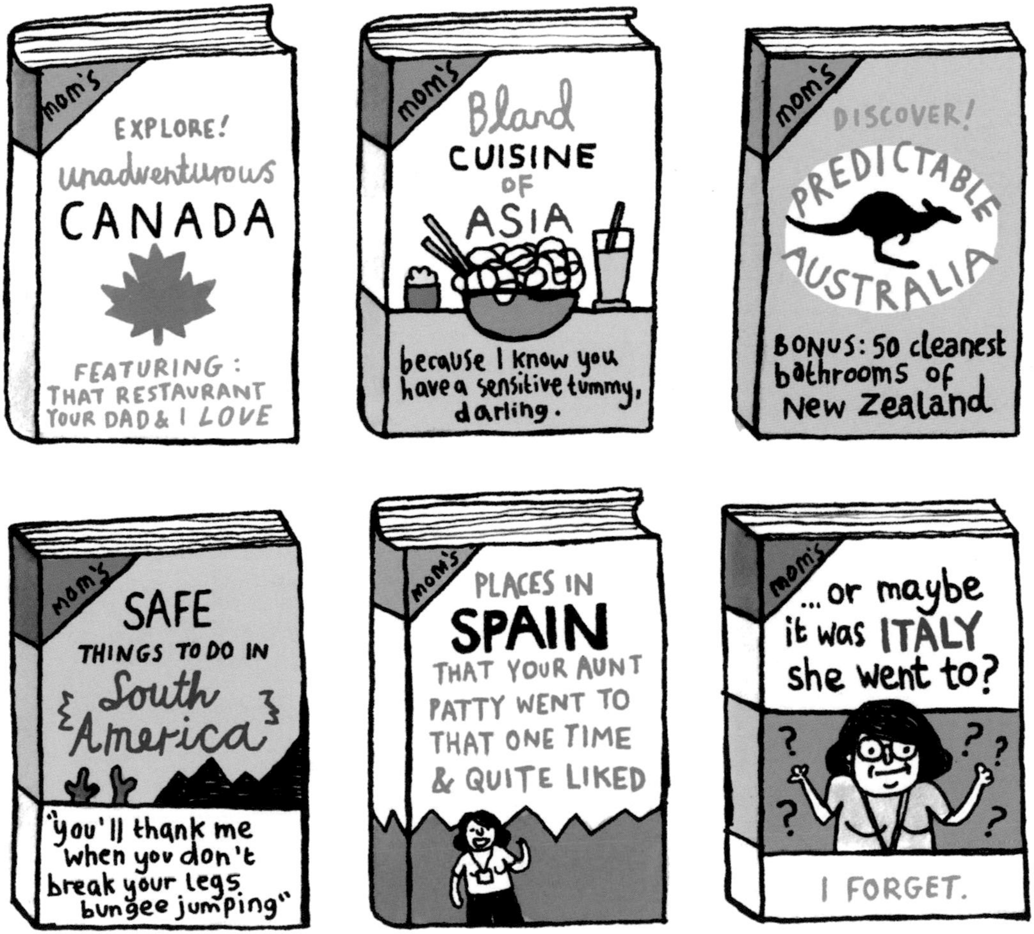
mom's
EXPLORE!
unadventurous
CANADA
FEATURING:
THAT RESTAURANT
YOUR DAD & I LOVE
mom's
Bland
CUISINE
OF
ASIA
because I know you
have a sensitive tummy,
darling.
mom's
DISCOVER!
PREDICTABLE
AUSTRALIA
BONUS: 50 cleanest
bathrooms of
New Zealand
mom's
SAFE
THINGS TO DO IN
South
America
"you'll thank me
when you don't
break your legs
bungee jumping"
mom's
PLACES IN
SPAIN
THAT YOUR AUNT
PATTY WENT TO
THAT ONE TIME
& QUITE LIKED
mom's
...or maybe
it was ITALY
she went to?
? ? ?
? ?
I FORGET.

ALSO AVAILABLE FROM PARENTAL PUBLISHING LTD:

DAD'S GOOD FOOD GUIDES:

" THE BEST ALL-YOU-CAN-EAT BUFFETS IN YOUR AREA"

& THE BESTSELLER "101 RESTAURANTS WITH FREE TOOTHPICKS"

LESS EXCITING BOARD GAMES FOR THE FAINT OF HEART

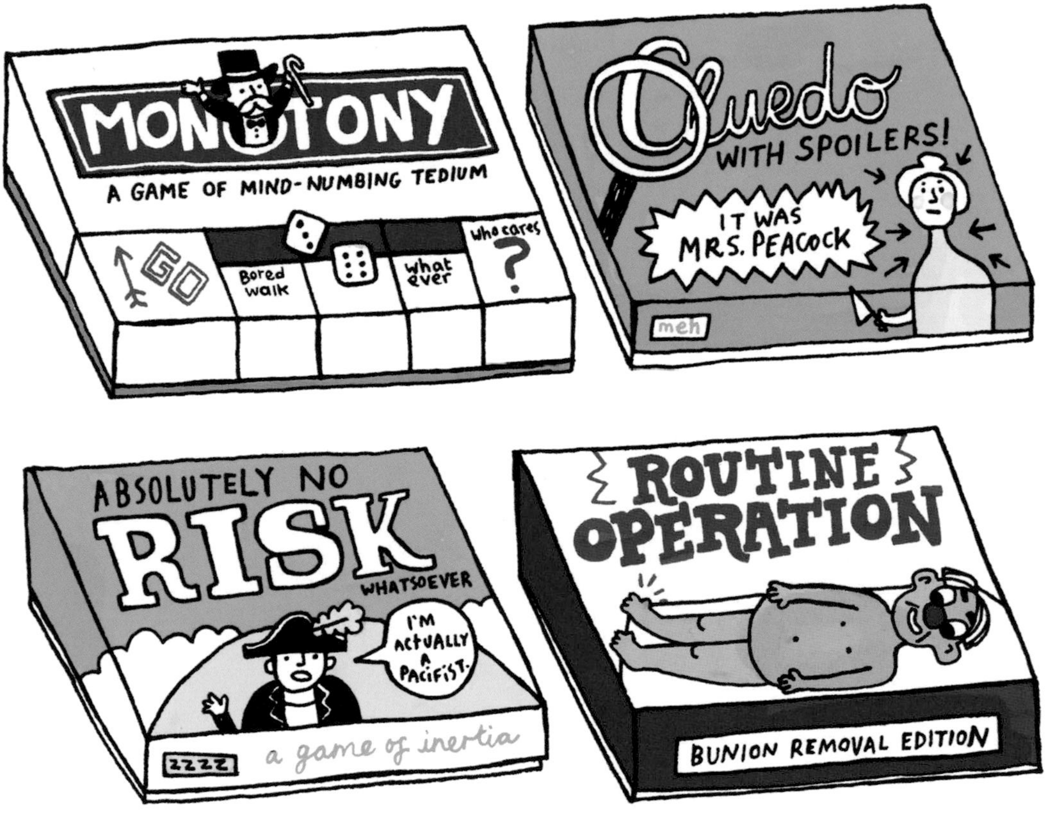
MONOTONY
A GAME OF MIND-NUMBING TEDIUM
GO
Bored walk
what ever
who cares
?
Cluedo
WITH SPOILERS!
IT WAS MRS. PEACOCK
meh
ABSOLUTELY NO
RISK
WHATSOEVER
I'M ACTUALLY A PACIFIST.
ZZZZ
a game of inertia
ROUTINE OPERATION
BUNION REMOVAL EDITION

ye Olde VIDEO GAMES

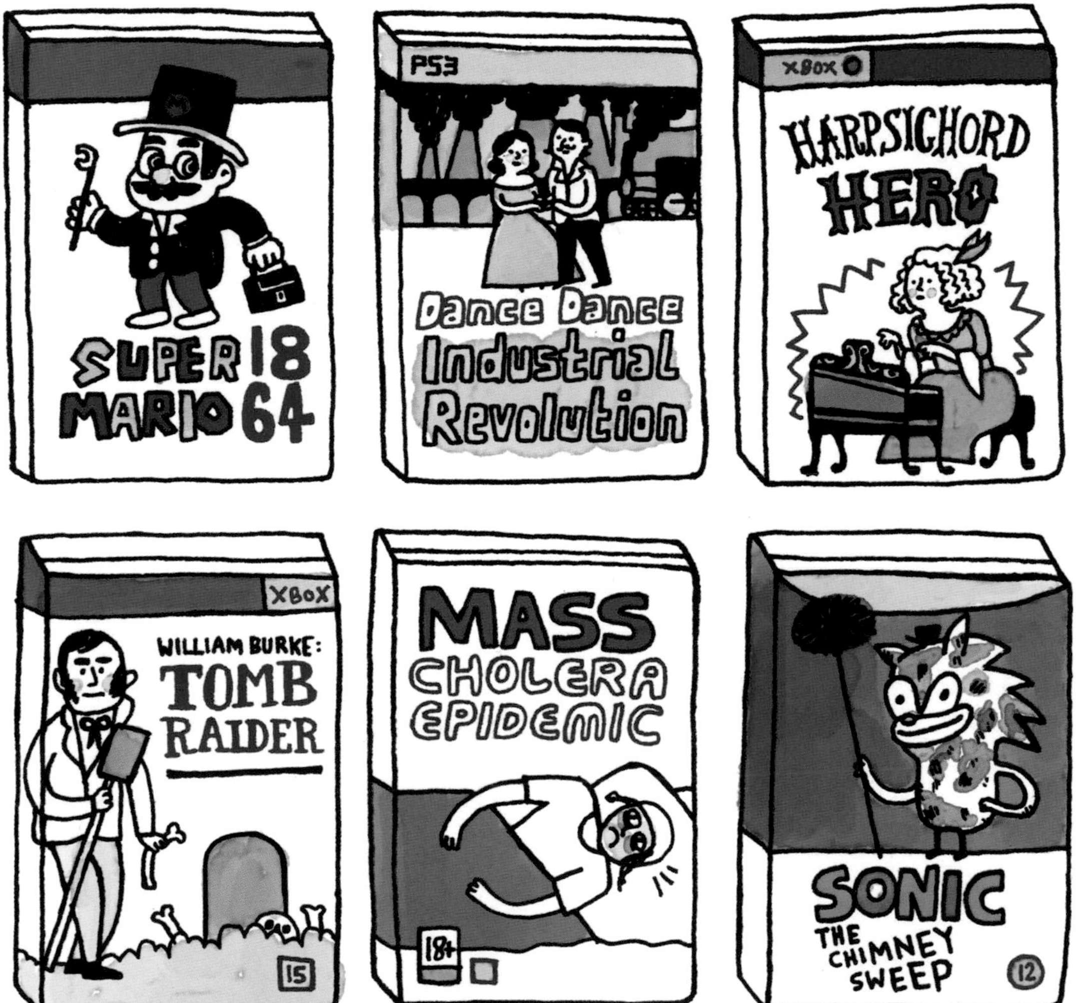
SUPER MARIO 1864
PS3
Dance Dance Industrial Revolution
XBOX
HARPSICHORD HERO
XBOX
WILLIAM BURKE: TOMB RAIDER
15
MASS CHOLERA EPIDEMIC
18+
SONIC THE CHIMNEY SWEEP
12

POPULAR GAME SHOWS OF THE DARK AGES

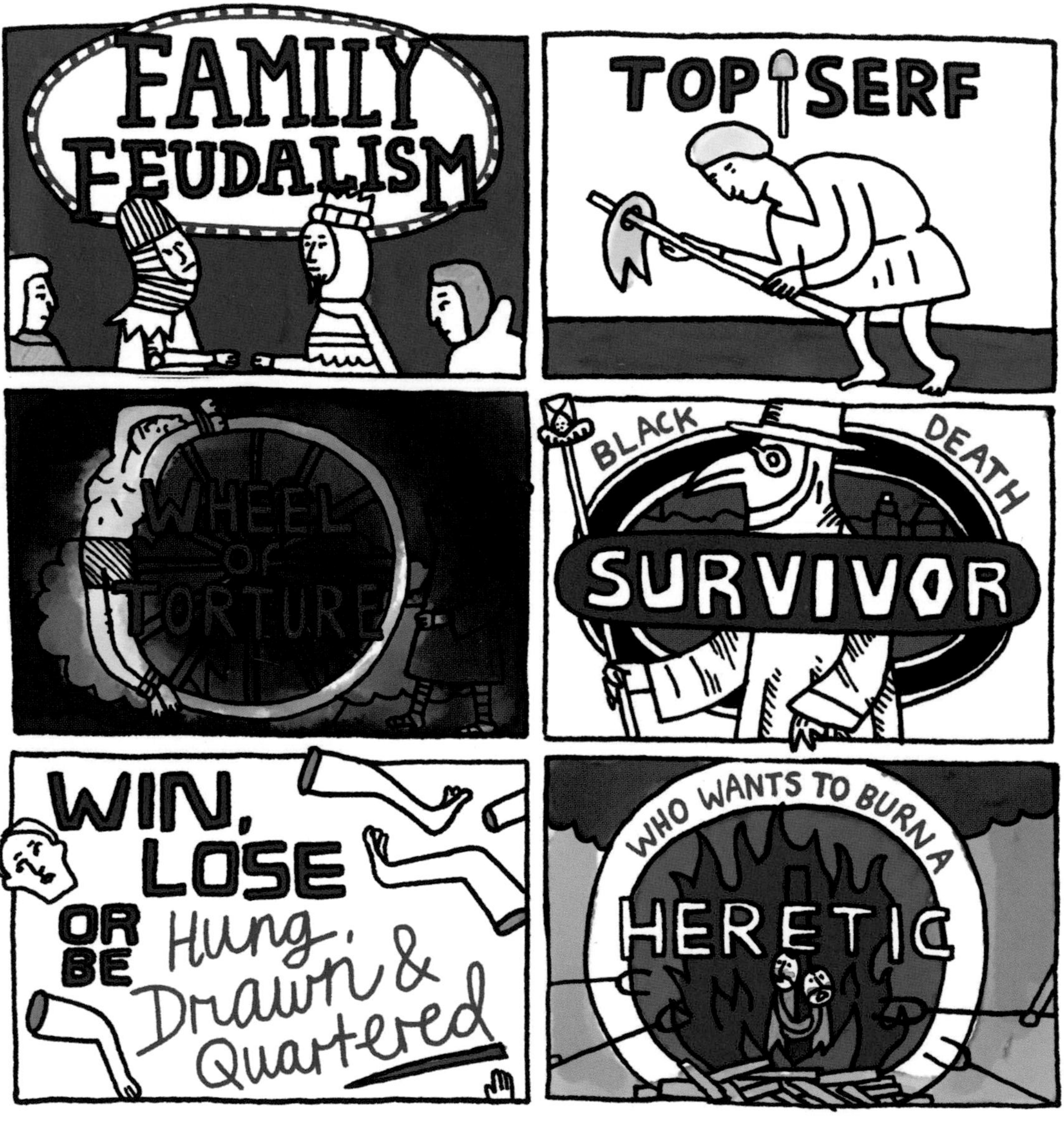
FAMILY FEUDALISM
TOP SERF
WHEEL OF TORTURE
BLACK DEATH
SURVIVOR
WIN, LOSE OR BE Hung, Drawn & Quartered
WHO WANTS TO BURN A
HERETIC

THIS SEASON ON

P·E·A·S·A·N·T·S

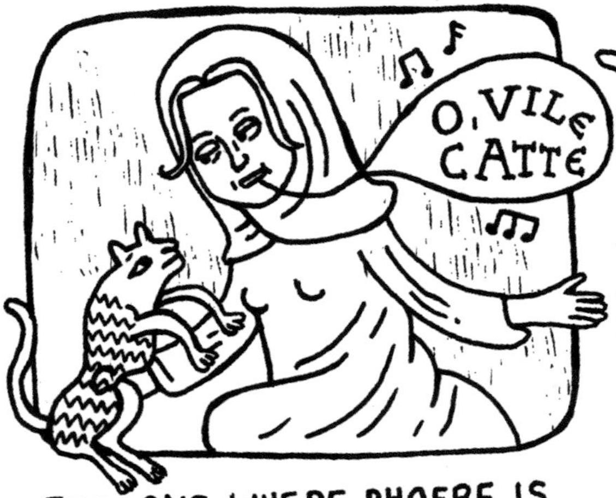
O, VILE
CATTE

THE ONE WHERE PHOEBE IS ACCUSED OF WITCHCRAFT

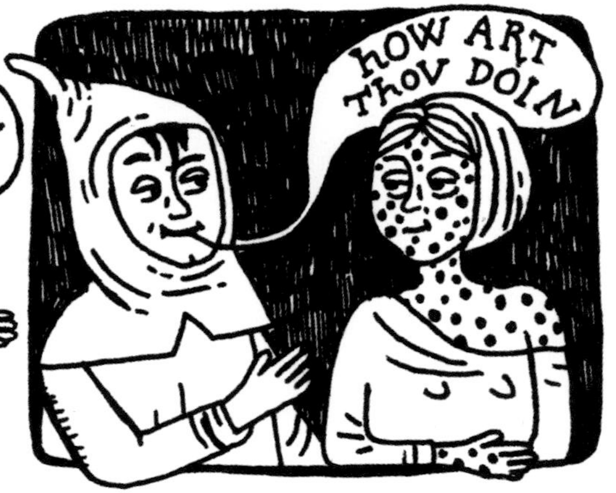
HOW ART
THOV DOIN

THE ONE WHERE JOEY IS AFFLICTED BY THE GREAT POX

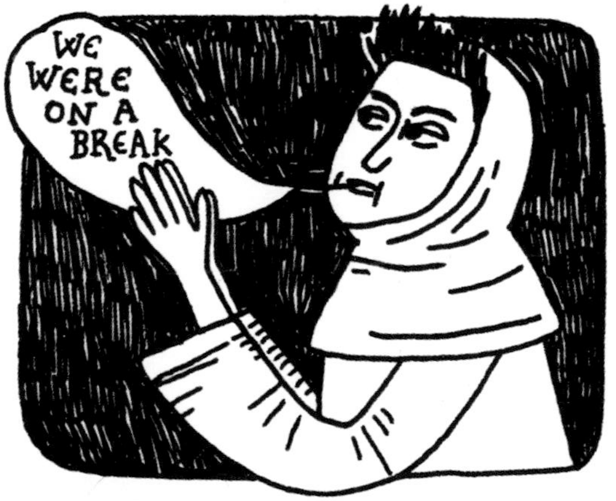
WE
WERE
ON A
BREAK

THE ONE WHERE ROSS DOES PENANCE FOR THE SIN OF FORNICATION

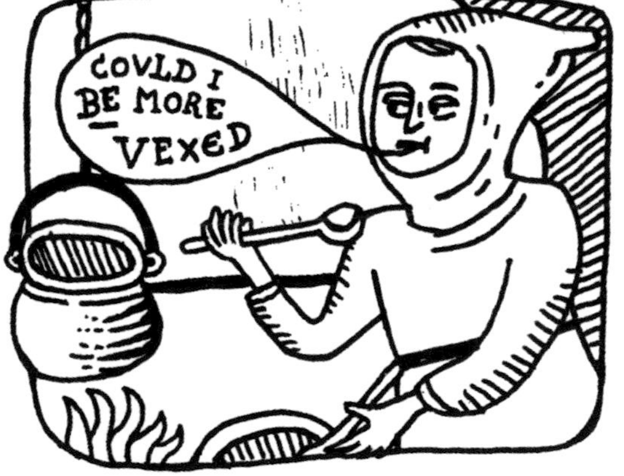
COVLD I
BE MORE
VEXED

THE ONE WITH ALL THE POTTAGE

MORE SEALIFE-THEMED DISASTER MOVIES

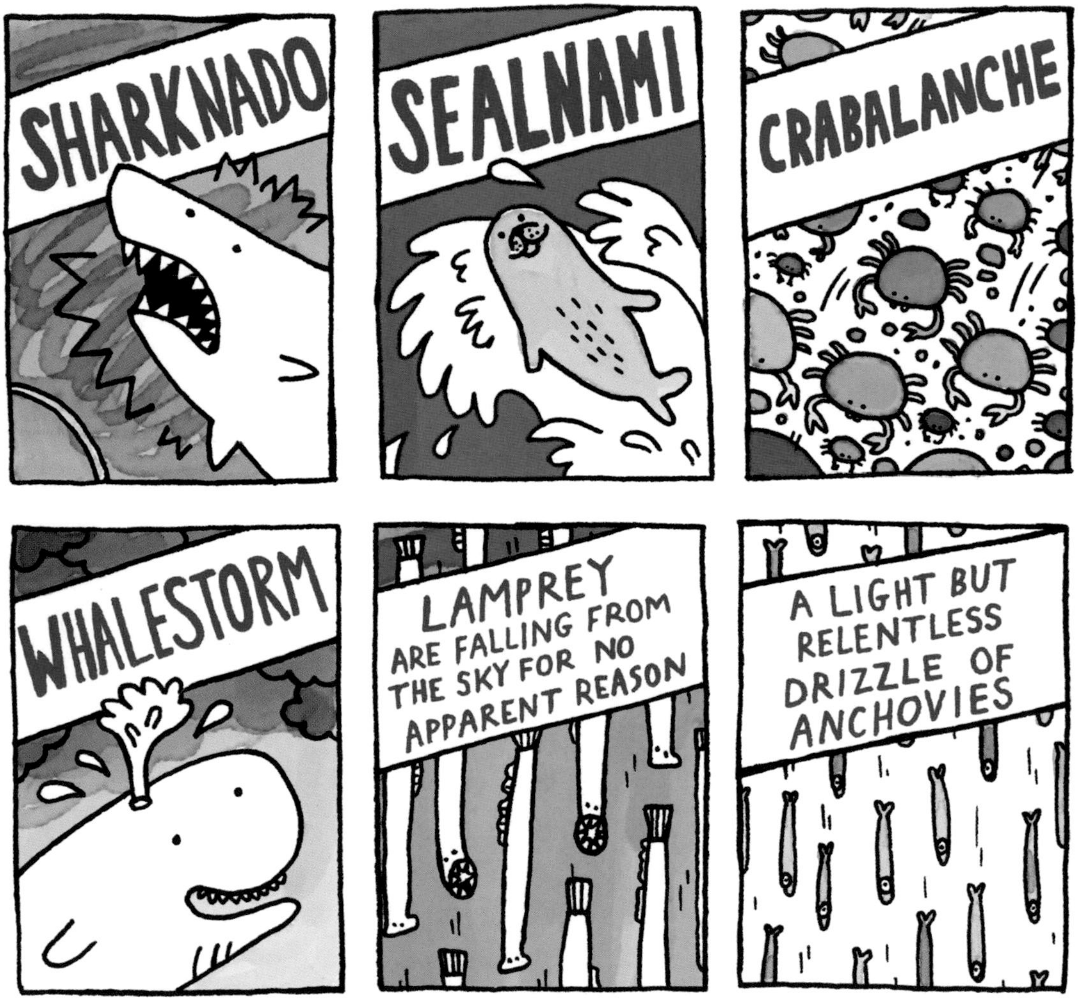
SHARKNADO
SEALNAMI
CRABALANCHE
WHALESTORM
LAMPREY ARE FALLING FROM THE SKY FOR NO APPARENT REASON
A LIGHT BUT RELENTLESS DRIZZLE OF ANCHOVIES

SUBURBAN GANGS

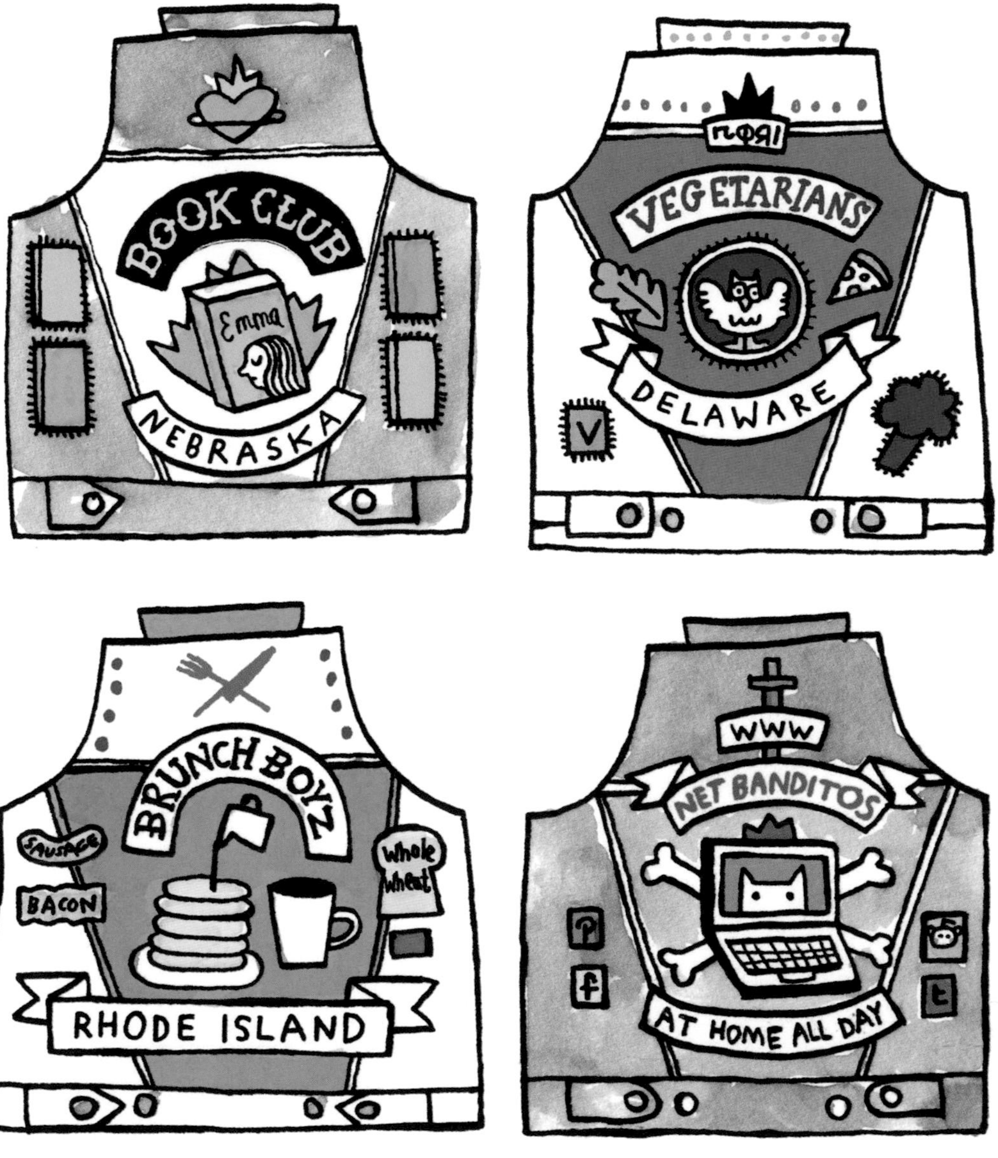
BOOK CLUB
Emma
NEBRASKA
VEGETARIANS
DELAWARE
V
BRUNCH BOYZ
SAUSAGE
BACON
Whole Wheat
RHODE ISLAND
WWW
NET BANDITOS
AT HOME ALL DAY

★★★ CHAPTER SEVEN ★★★

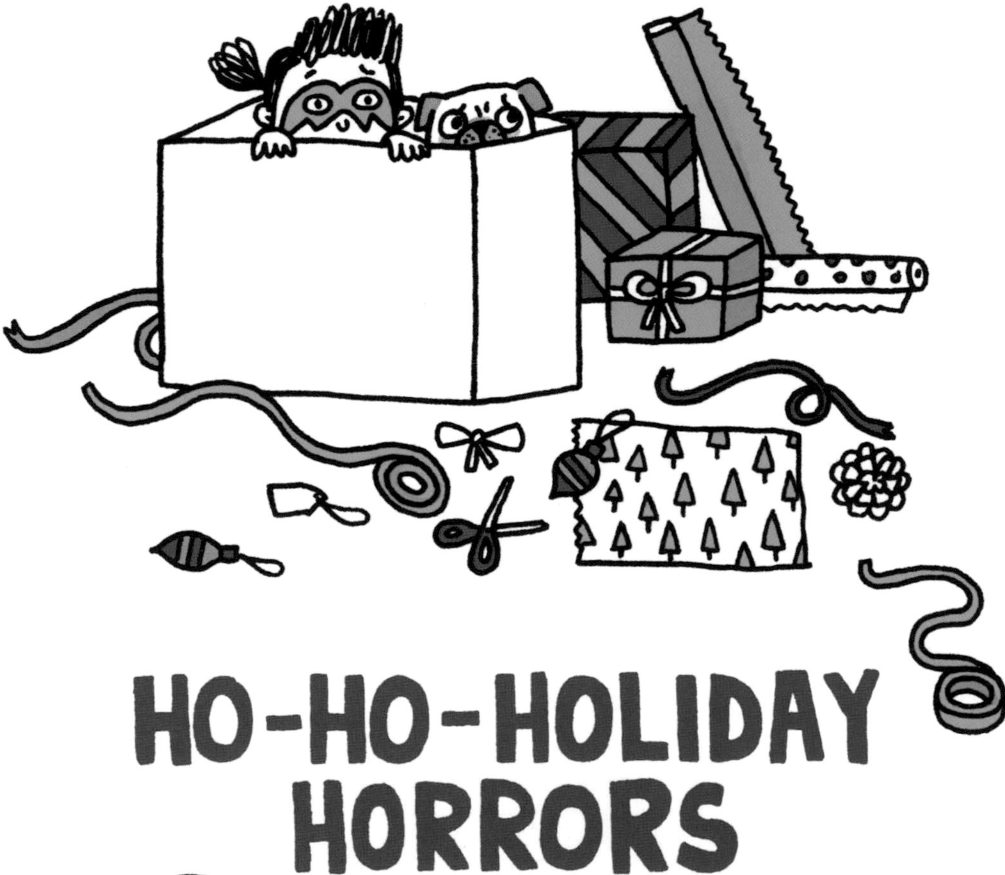

HO-HO-HOLIDAY HORRORS

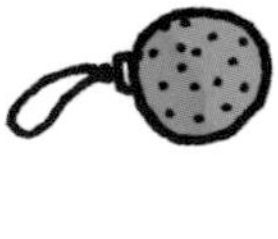

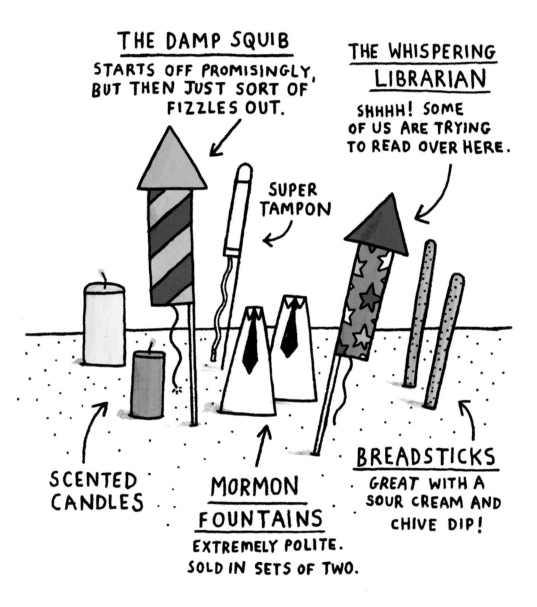

FIREWORKS FOR THE FAINT OF HEART

THE DAMP SQUIB
STARTS OFF PROMISINGLY,
BUT THEN JUST SORT OF
FIZZLES OUT.

THE WHISPERING
LIBRARIAN
SHHHH! SOME
OF US ARE TRYING
TO READ OVER HERE.

SUPER
TAMPON

SCENTED
CANDLES

MORMON
FOUNTAINS
EXTREMELY POLITE.
SOLD IN SETS OF TWO.

BREADSTICKS
GREAT WITH A
SOUR CREAM AND
CHIVE DIP!

GHOST FASHIONS

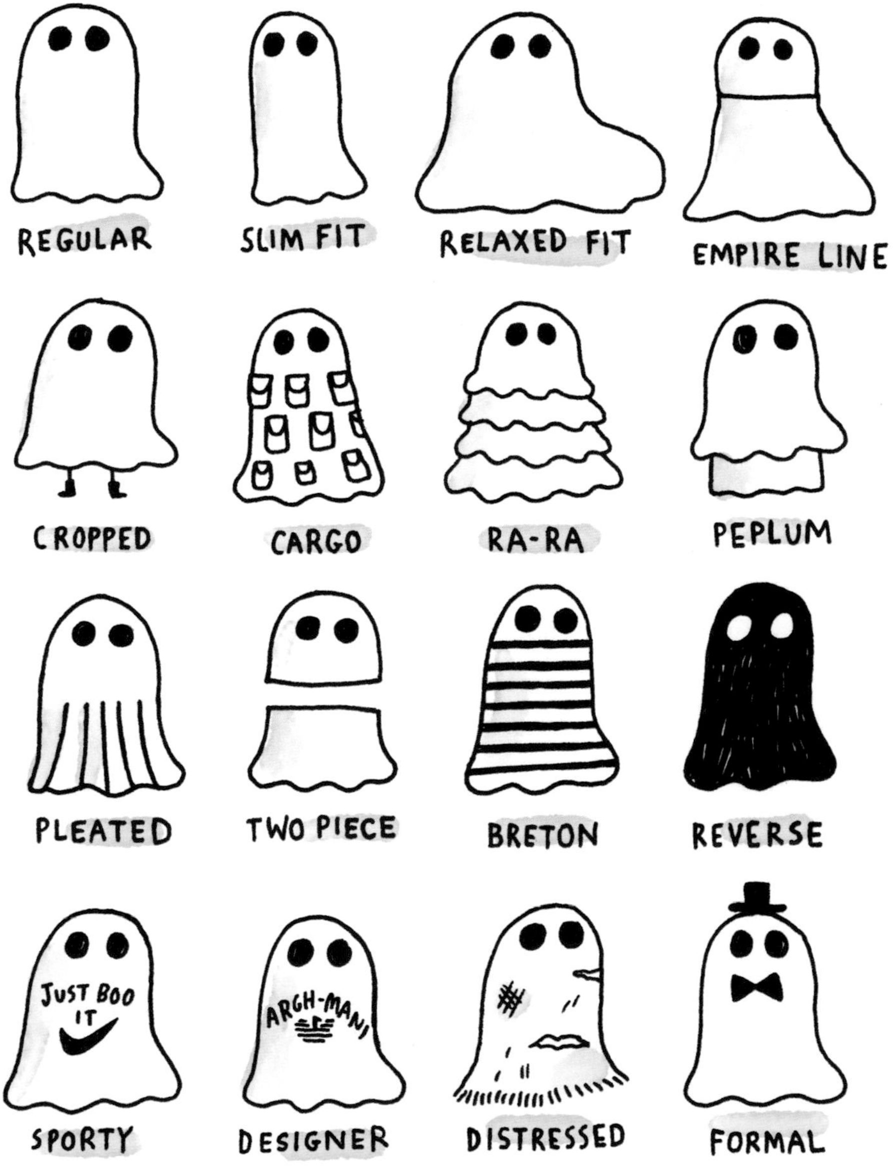
REGULAR
SLIM FIT
RELAXED FIT
EMPIRE LINE
CROPPED
CARGO
RA-RA
PEPLUM
PLEATED
TWO PIECE
BRETON
REVERSE
JUST BOO IT
SPORTY
ARGH-MANI
DESIGNER
DISTRESSED
FORMAL

SEXY HALLOWEEN COSTUMES FOR THE LAYDEEZ

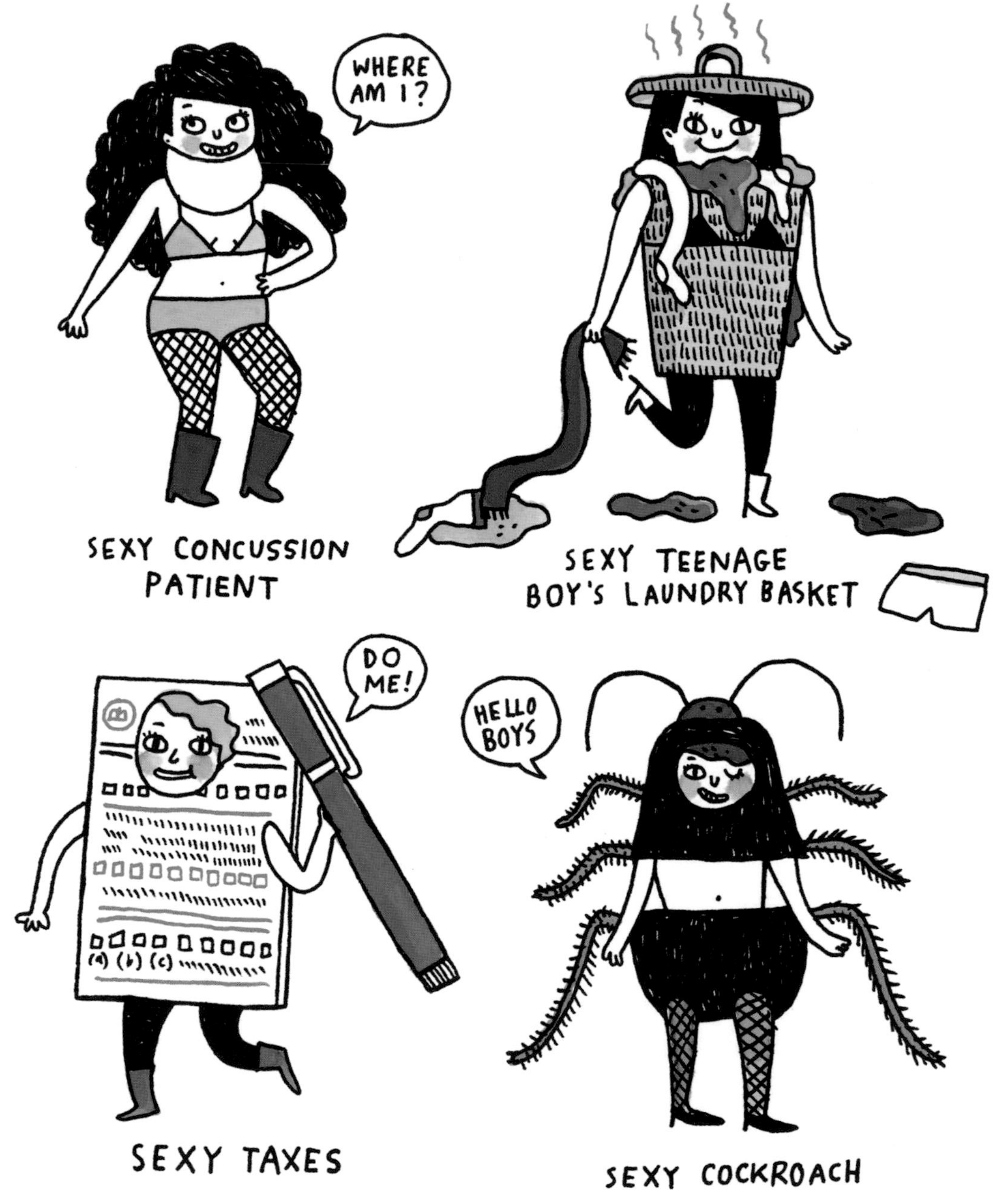
WHERE AM I?
SEXY CONCUSSION PATIENT
SEXY TEENAGE BOY'S LAUNDRY BASKET
DO ME!
SEXY TAXES
HELLO BOYS
SEXY COCKROACH

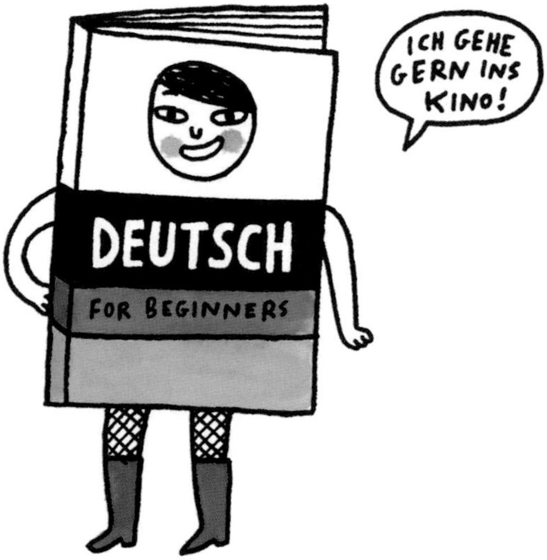
DEUTSCH
FOR BEGINNERS
ICH GEHE GERN INS KINO!

SEXY GERMAN TEXTBOOK

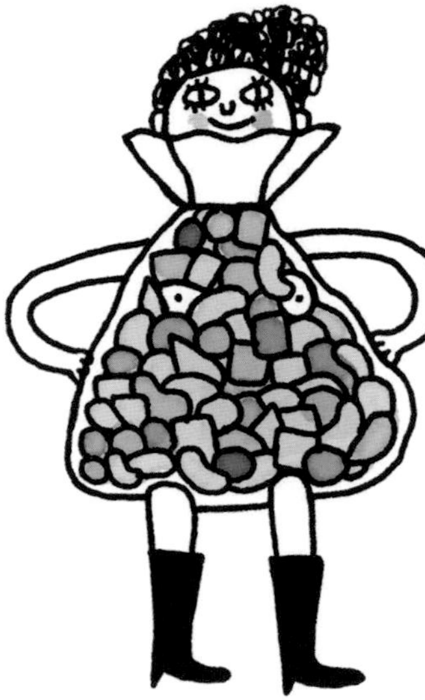

SEXY TRAIL MIX

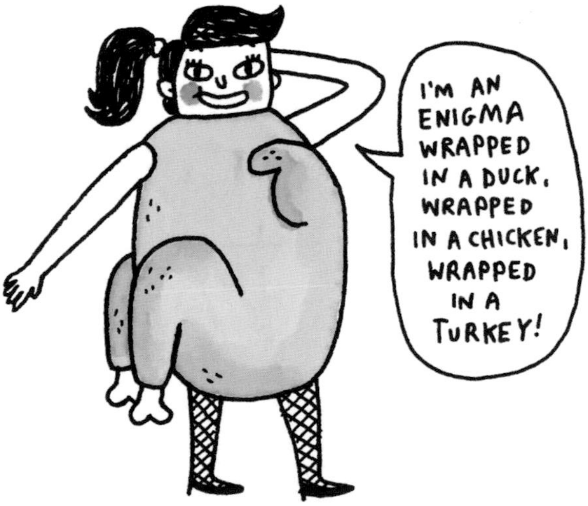
I'M AN ENIGMA WRAPPED IN A DUCK, WRAPPED IN A CHICKEN, WRAPPED IN A TURKEY!

SEXY TURDUCKEN

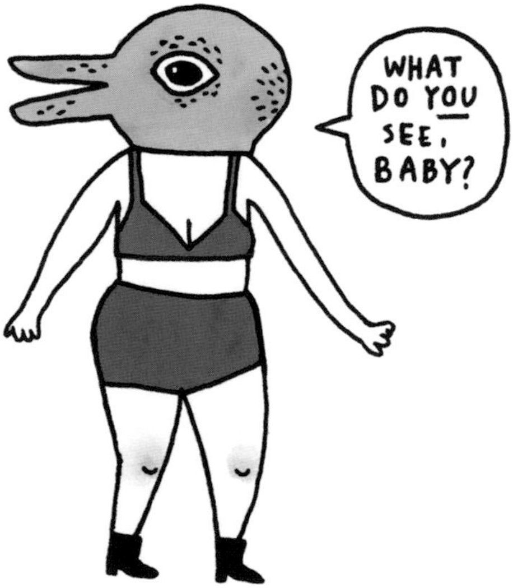
WHAT DO YOU SEE, BABY?

SEXY PARADIGM SHIFT

HOW TO DRAW A TURKEY

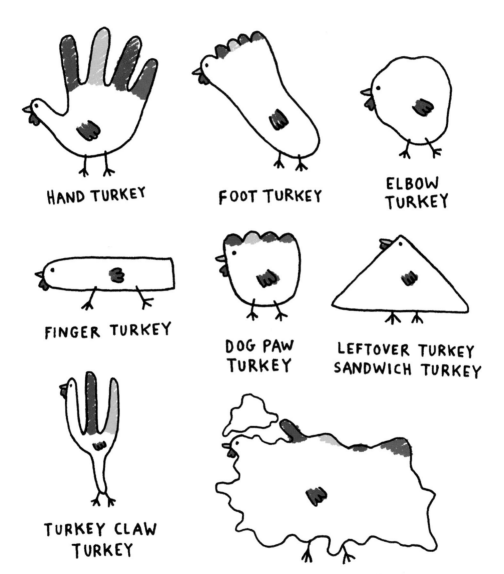

HAND TURKEY

FOOT TURKEY

ELBOW TURKEY

FINGER TURKEY

DOG PAW TURKEY

LEFTOVER TURKEY SANDWICH TURKEY

TURKEY CLAW TURKEY

BADLY DRAWN MAP OF TURKEY TURKEY

LESS APPEALING SEASONAL DRINKS

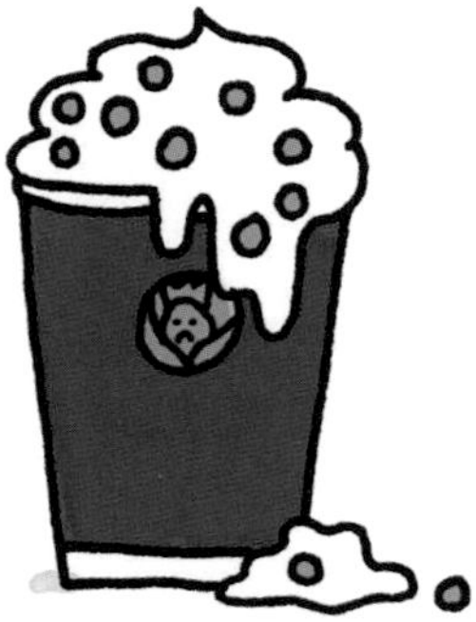

MASHED POTATO LATTE
(WITH OR WITHOUT PEAS)

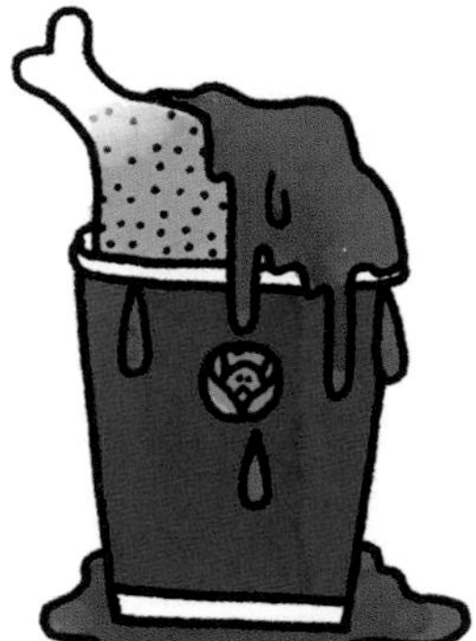

TURKEY & GRAVY MACCHIATO

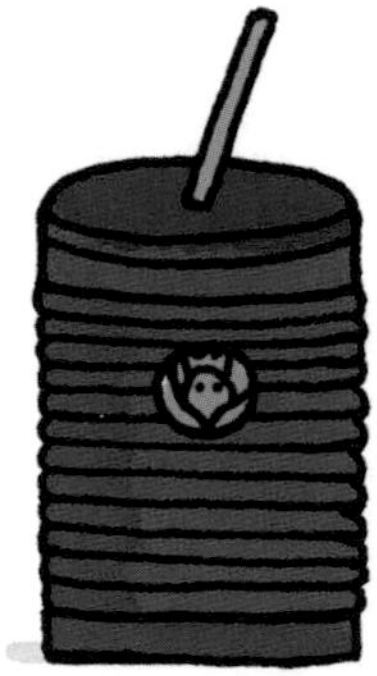

CRANBERRY SAUCE FROM A CAN, WITH A STRAW IN IT

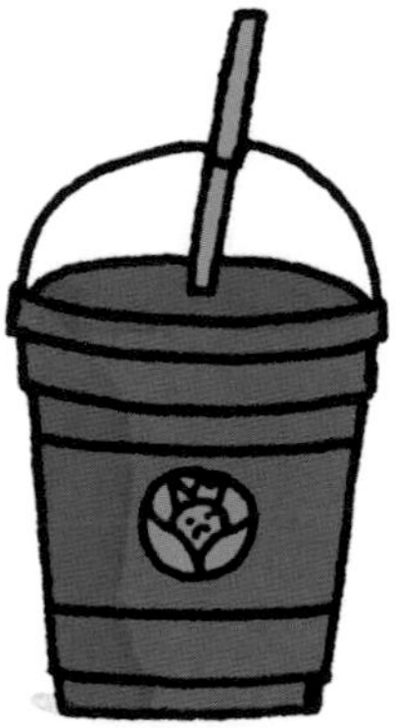

COUGH SYRUP FRAPPUCCINO

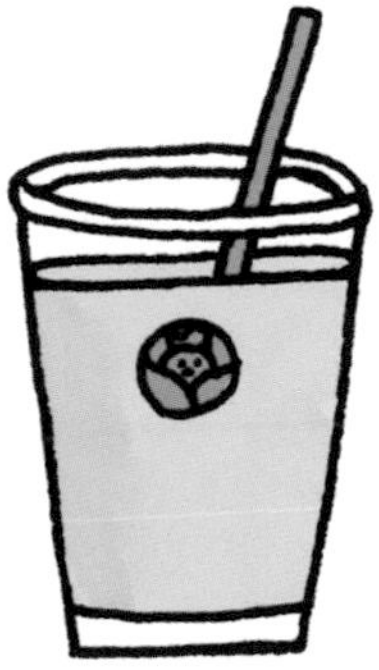

YELLOW SNOW ICED TEA

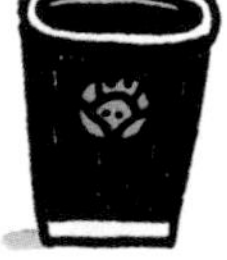

SEASONAL AFFECTIVE DISORDER ESPRESSO

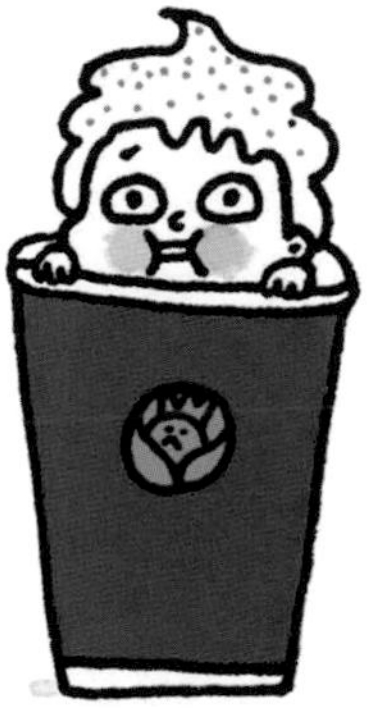

ANNE GEDDES BABYCCINO

FESTIVE SCENTS

Christmas SPICE
Gingerbread COOKIES
Simmering TENSIONS
mulled WINE
mild PANIC
PEPPERMINT PATTIE
Overboiled SPROUTS
Spilled EGGNOG
Existential DESPAIR

ALTERNATIVE CHRISTMAS TREES

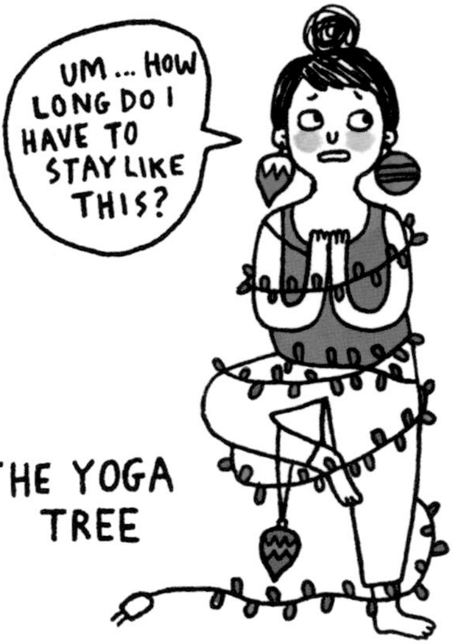
UM ... HOW LONG DO I HAVE TO STAY LIKE THIS?

THE YOGA TREE

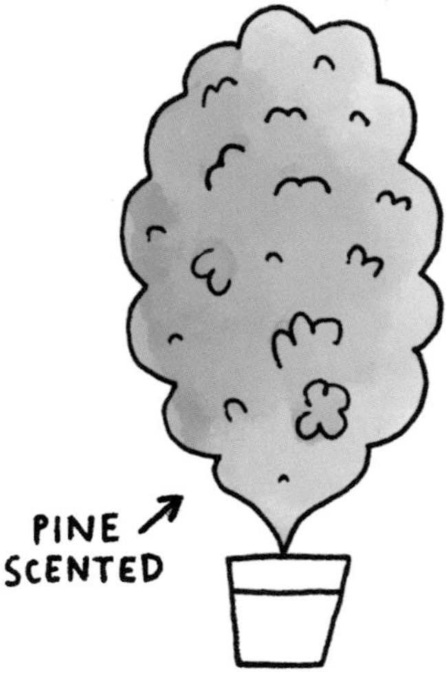
PINE SCENTED

THE AROMATHERATREE

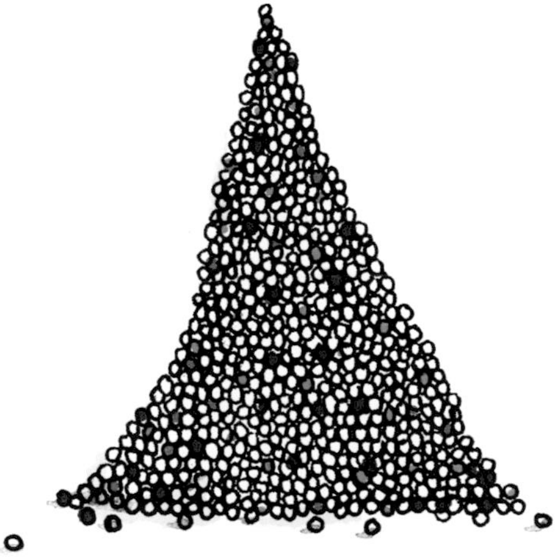

THE VITAMIN TREE

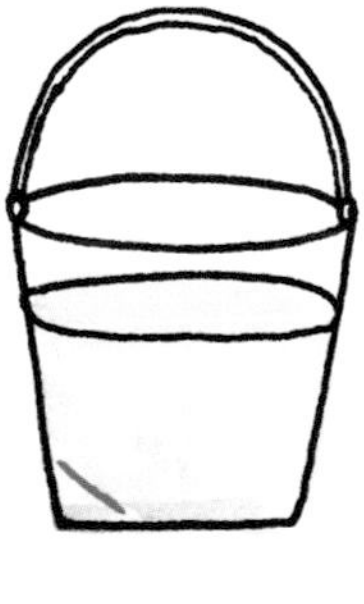

THE HOMEOPATHIC TREE
(A SINGLE PINE NEEDLE IN A BUCKET OF WATER)

CHAPTER EIGHT

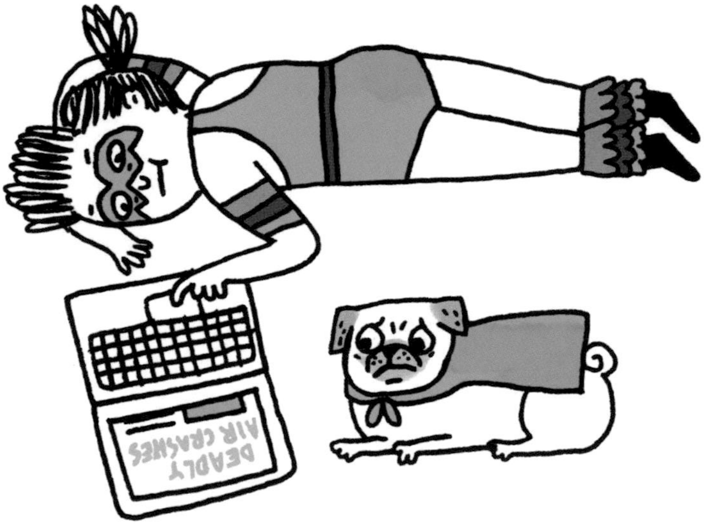
DEADLY
AIR CRASHES

MODERN MALAISES

NEWLY DISCOVERED CONSTELLATIONS

THE RENT HIKE (MAJOR)

(MINOR)

THE DISCARDED CAPPUCCINO

THE TAKE-OUT MENU

THE OVER-PRICED CUPCAKE

THE QUESTIONABLE BURRITO

THE BROKEN UMBRELLA

THE OVERCROWDED SUBWAY CAR

THE RAT

THE ACHING MELANCHOLY

THE IRRITATING BUSKER

THE RIDICULOUSLY LONG BRUNCH LINE

THE LACK OF PERSONAL SPACE

MODERN CURSES

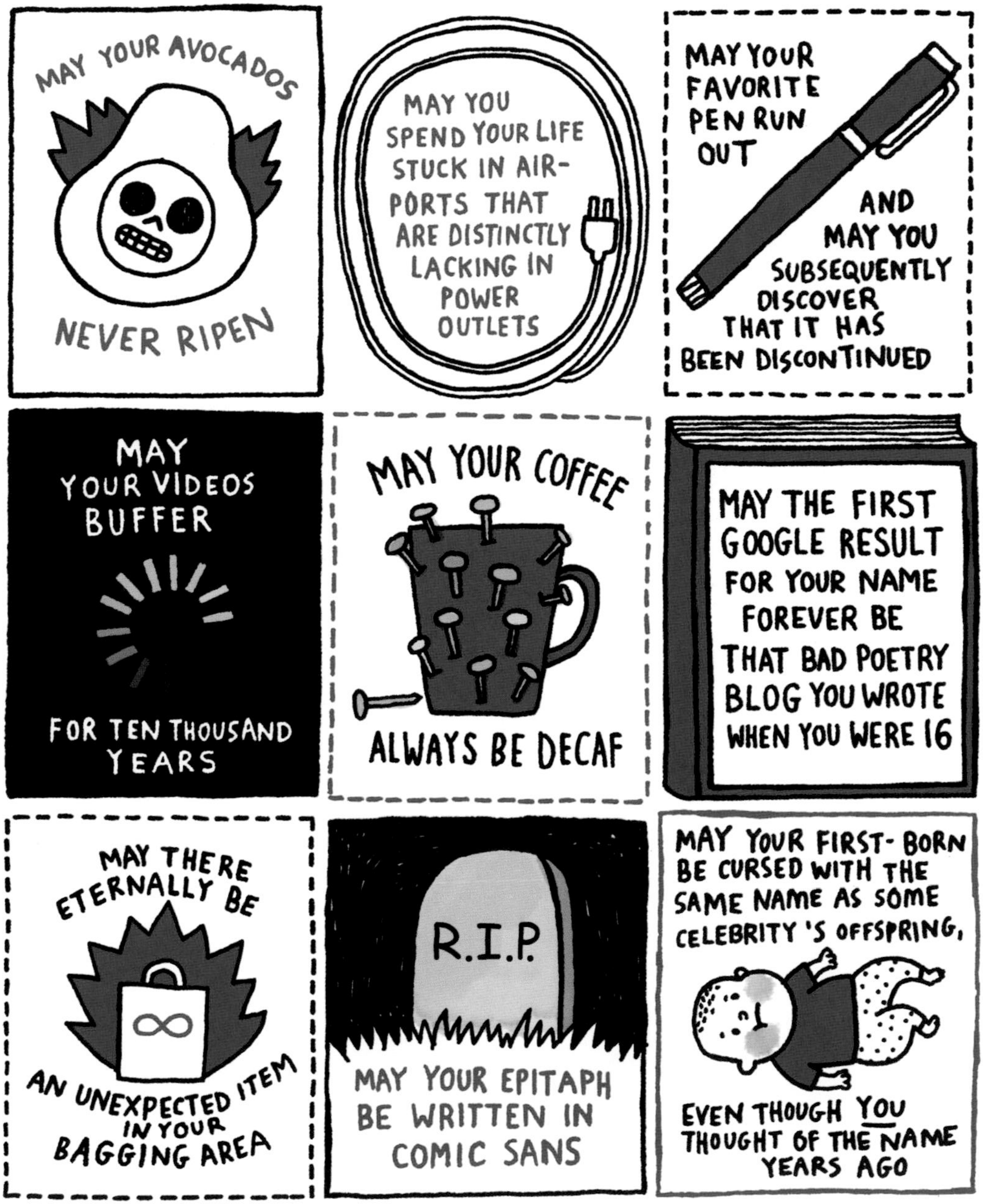
MAY YOUR AVOCADOS NEVER RIPEN
MAY YOU SPEND YOUR LIFE STUCK IN AIRPORTS THAT ARE DISTINCTLY LACKING IN POWER OUTLETS
MAY YOUR FAVORITE PEN RUN OUT AND MAY YOU SUBSEQUENTLY DISCOVER THAT IT HAS BEEN DISCONTINUED
MAY YOUR VIDEOS BUFFER FOR TEN THOUSAND YEARS
MAY YOUR COFFEE ALWAYS BE DECAF
MAY THE FIRST GOOGLE RESULT FOR YOUR NAME FOREVER BE THAT BAD POETRY BLOG YOU WROTE WHEN YOU WERE 16
MAY THERE ETERNALLY BE AN UNEXPECTED ITEM IN YOUR BAGGING AREA
R.I.P.
MAY YOUR EPITAPH BE WRITTEN IN COMIC SANS
MAY YOUR FIRST-BORN BE CURSED WITH THE SAME NAME AS SOME CELEBRITY'S OFFSPRING,
EVEN THOUGH YOU THOUGHT OF THE NAME YEARS AGO

INTERNATIONAL LANDLUBBER CODE FLAGS

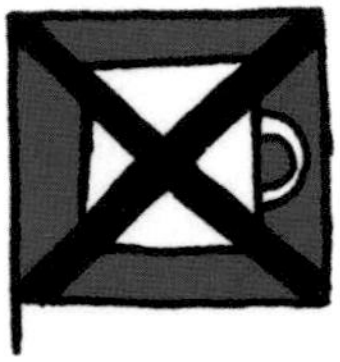

"CAUTION: UNCAFFEINATED."

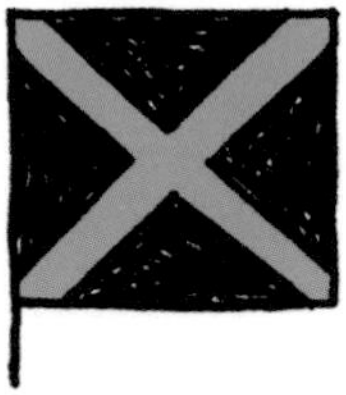

"I DO NOT WISH TO COMMUNICATE WITH YOU."

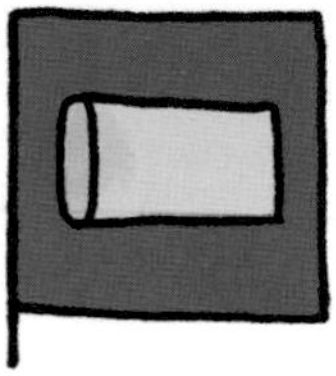

"I REQUIRE A BURRITO."

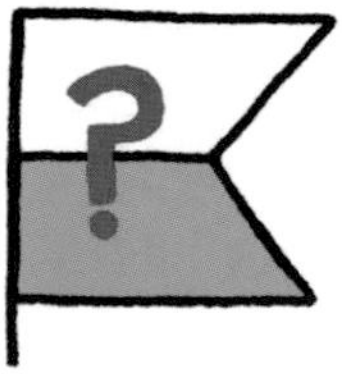

"I HAVE NO IDEA WHAT I'M DOING."

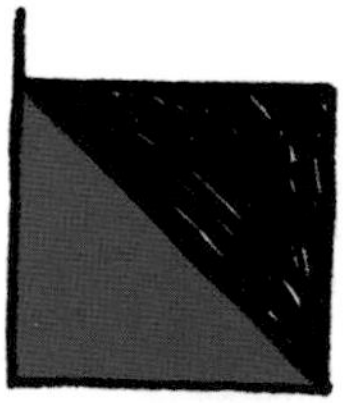

"I AM DRUNK."

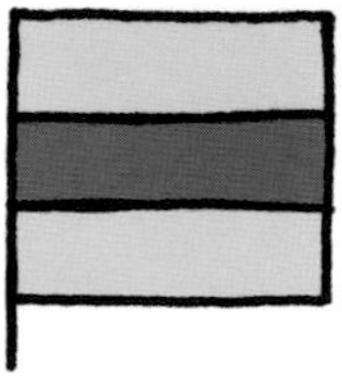

"I AM ON FIRE." (FIGURATIVELY)

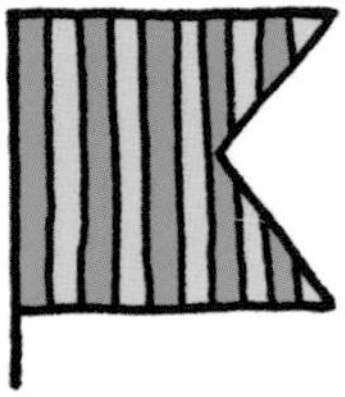

"I REQUIRE FRIES WITH THAT."

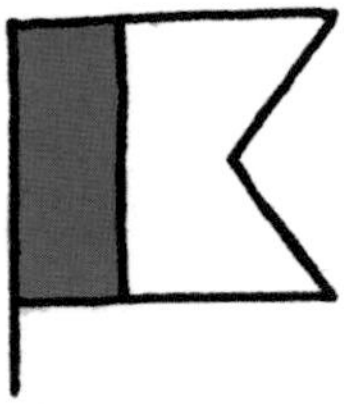

"LEAVE ME ALONE."

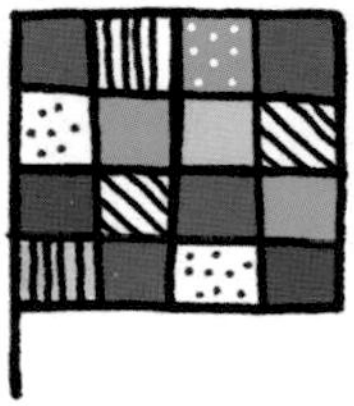

"PLEASE VISIT MY ETSY SHOP."

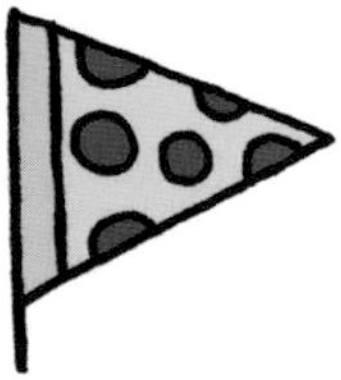

"I AM ALTERING MY COURSE TO THE NEAREST PIZZA PLACE."

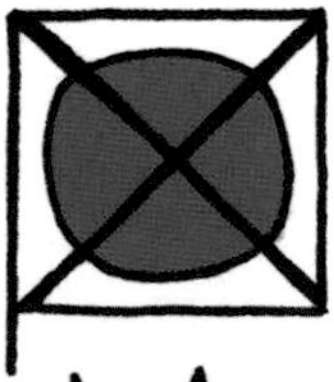

"KEEP CLEAR: I HAVE P.M.S."

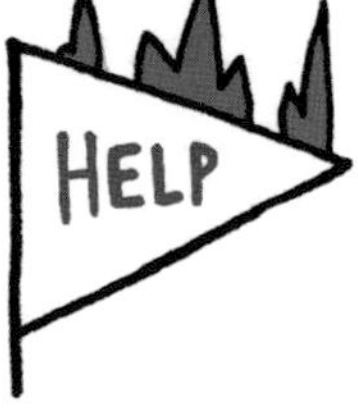
HELP

"I AM ON FIRE." (LITERALLY)

ADVANCED MOOD RING READING

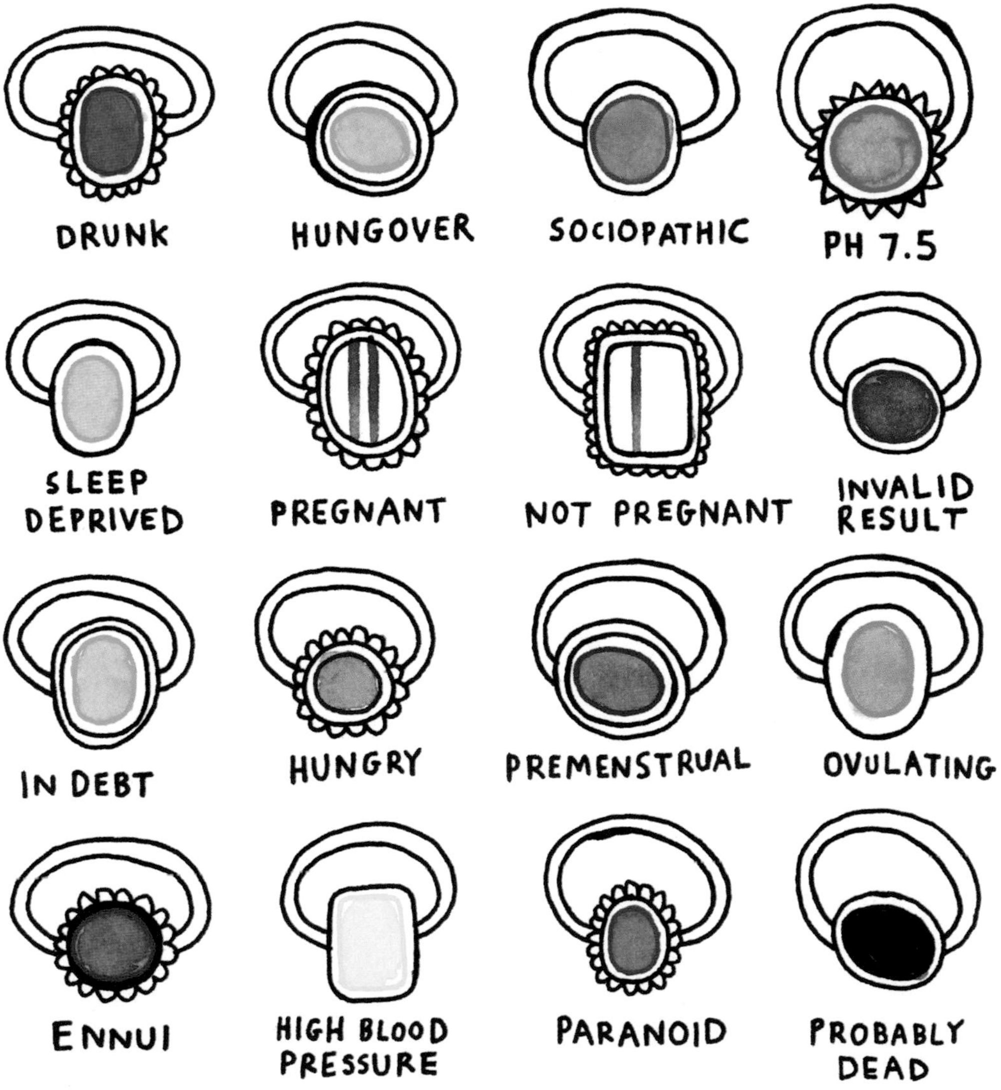
DRUNK
HUNGOVER
SOCIOPATHIC
PH 7.5
SLEEP DEPRIVED
PREGNANT
NOT PREGNANT
INVALID RESULT
IN DEBT
HUNGRY
PREMENSTRUAL
OVULATING
ENNUI
HIGH BLOOD PRESSURE
PARANOID
PROBABLY DEAD

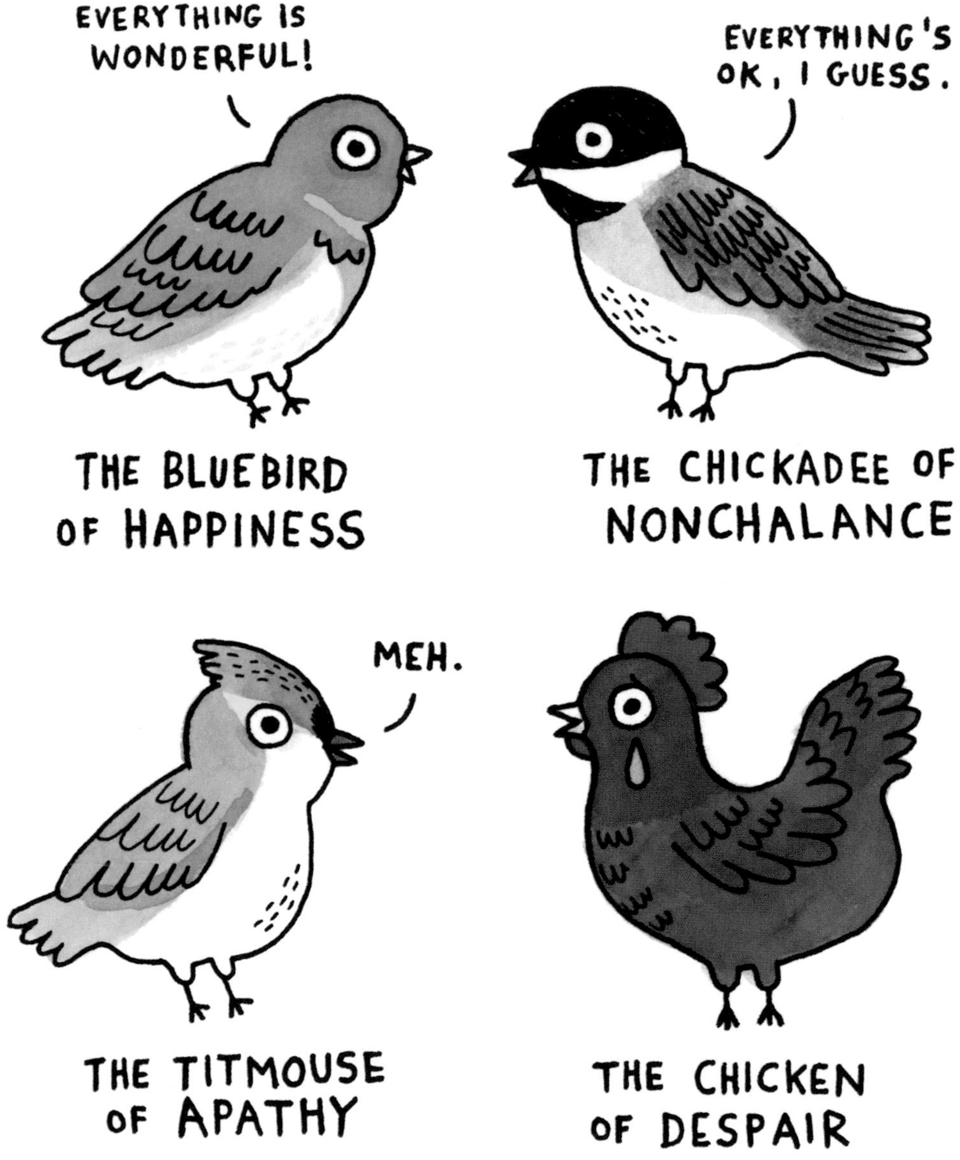
EVERYTHING IS WONDERFUL!
THE BLUEBIRD OF HAPPINESS
EVERYTHING'S OK, I GUESS.
THE CHICKADEE OF NONCHALANCE
MEH.
THE TITMOUSE OF APATHY
THE CHICKEN OF DESPAIR

SIGNS OF THE DYSTOPIAN ZODIAC

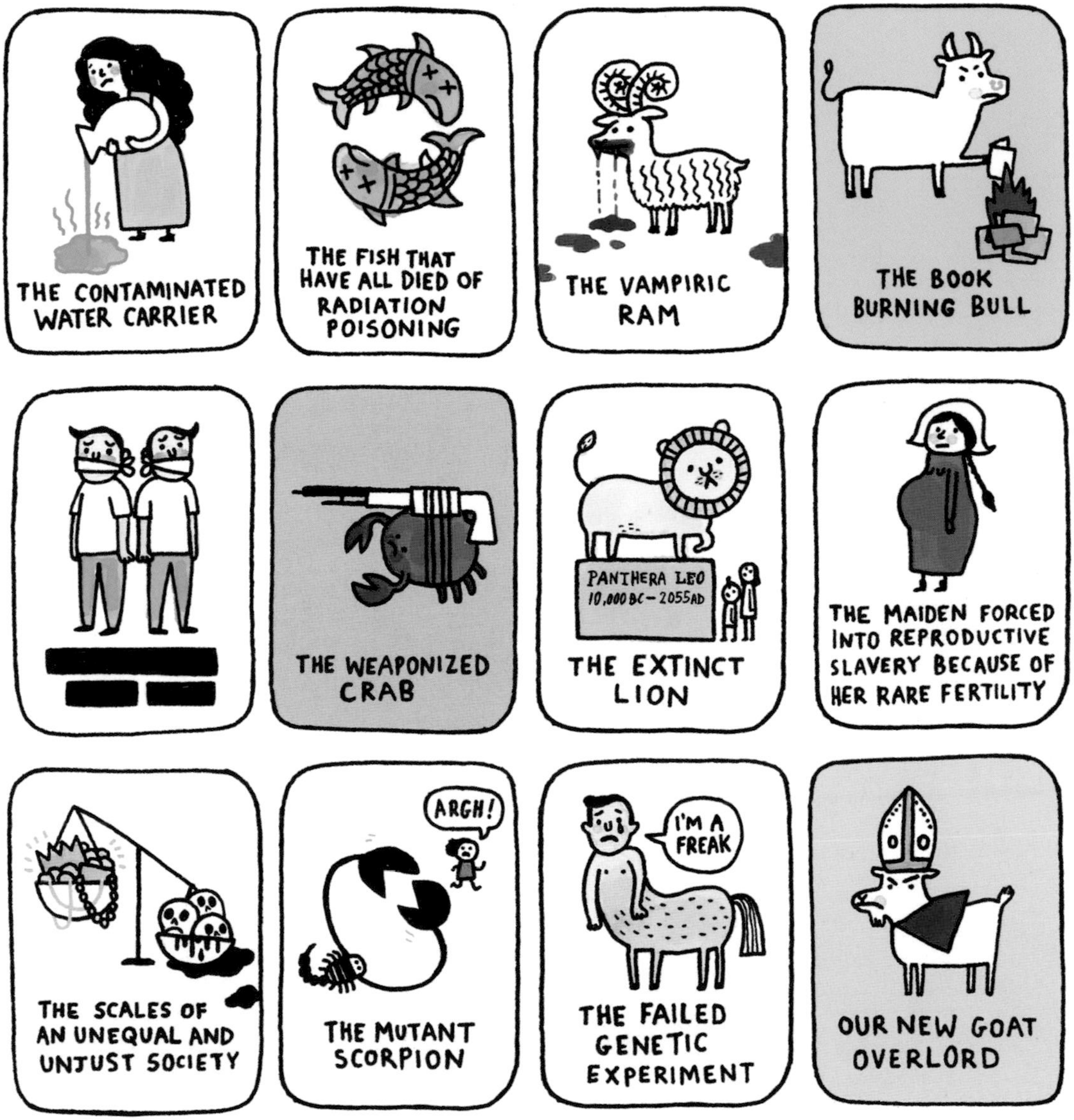
THE CONTAMINATED WATER CARRIER
THE FISH THAT HAVE ALL DIED OF RADIATION POISONING
THE VAMPIRIC RAM
THE BOOK BURNING BULL
THE WEAPONIZED CRAB
PANTHERA LEO 10,000 BC – 2055 AD
THE EXTINCT LION
THE MAIDEN FORCED INTO REPRODUCTIVE SLAVERY BECAUSE OF HER RARE FERTILITY
THE SCALES OF AN UNEQUAL AND UNJUST SOCIETY
ARGH!
THE MUTANT SCORPION
I'M A FREAK
THE FAILED GENETIC EXPERIMENT
OUR NEW GOAT OVERLORD

NON-BIBLICAL PLAGUES

PLAGUE OF FRAPPUCCINOS

PLAGUE OF UGGS

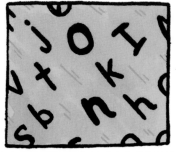
PLAGUE OF COMIC SANS

PLAGUE OF OVERCOOKED PASTA

PLAGUE OF HASHTAGS

PLAGUE OF KALE

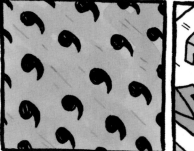
PLAGUE OF MISPLACED
APOSTROPHES

PLAGUE OF V-NECKS

PLAGUE OF KARDASHIANS

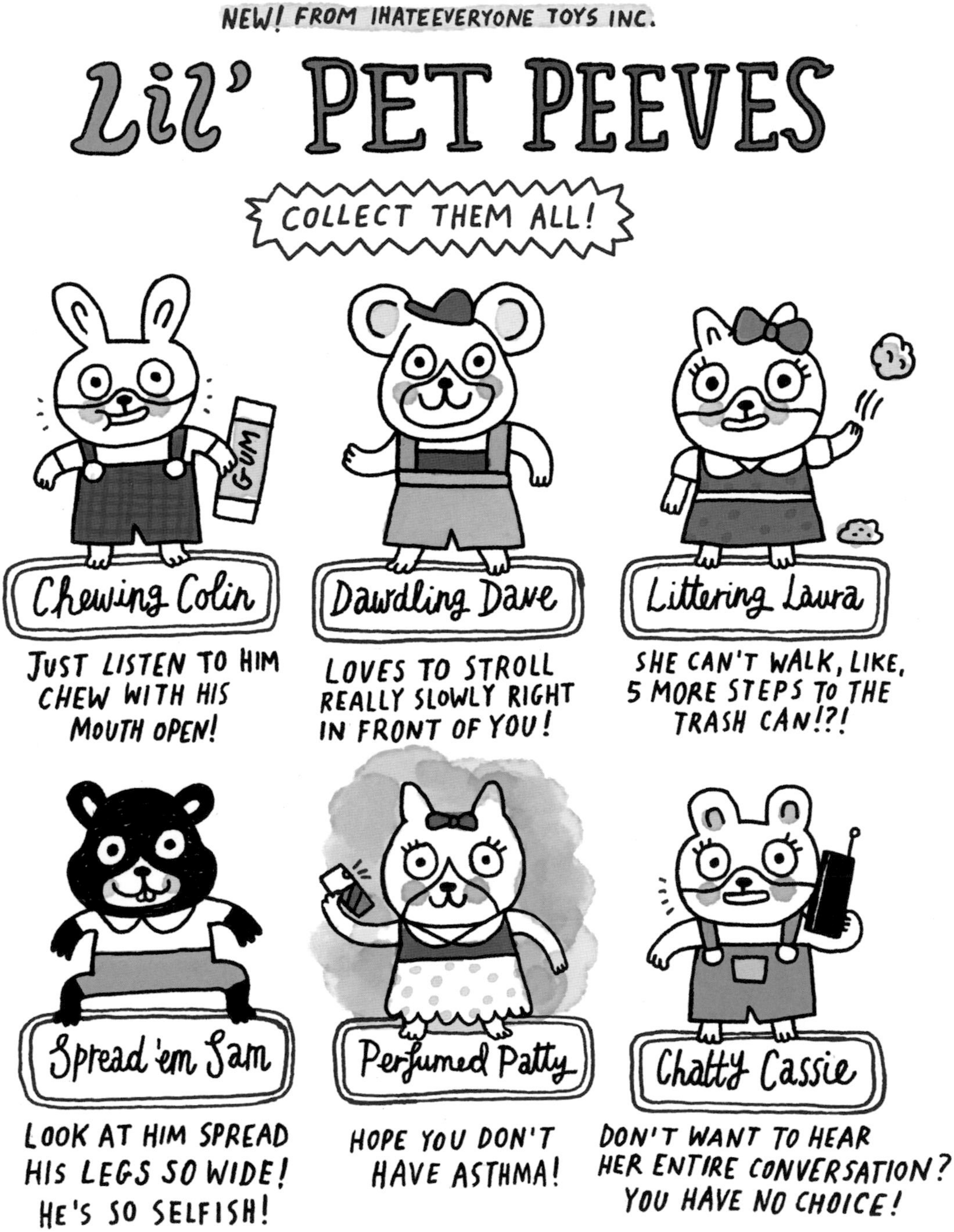
NEW! FROM IHATEEVERYONE TOYS INC.
Lil' PET PEEVES
COLLECT THEM ALL!
GUM
Chewing Colin
JUST LISTEN TO HIM CHEW WITH HIS MOUTH OPEN!
Dawdling Dave
LOVES TO STROLL REALLY SLOWLY RIGHT IN FRONT OF YOU!
Littering Laura
SHE CAN'T WALK, LIKE, 5 MORE STEPS TO THE TRASH CAN!?!
Spread 'em Sam
LOOK AT HIM SPREAD HIS LEGS SO WIDE! HE'S SO SELFISH!
Perfumed Patty
HOPE YOU DON'T HAVE ASTHMA!
Chatty Cassie
DON'T WANT TO HEAR HER ENTIRE CONVERSATION? YOU HAVE NO CHOICE!

THE LATEST IN WEARABLE TECHNOLOGIES

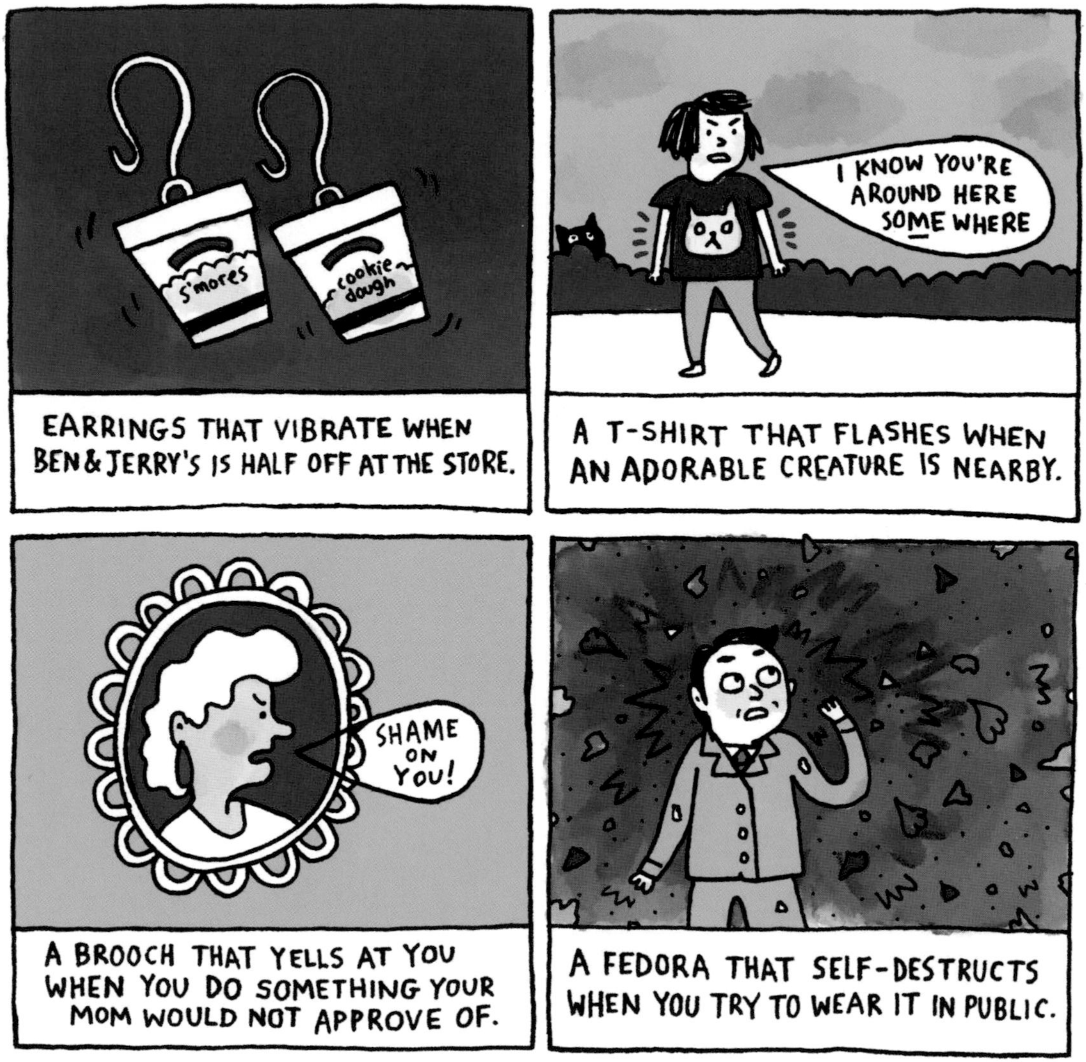

S'mores
cookie dough
EARRINGS THAT VIBRATE WHEN BEN & JERRY'S IS HALF OFF AT THE STORE.
I KNOW YOU'RE AROUND HERE SOMEWHERE
A T-SHIRT THAT FLASHES WHEN AN ADORABLE CREATURE IS NEARBY.
SHAME ON YOU!
A BROOCH THAT YELLS AT YOU WHEN YOU DO SOMETHING YOUR MOM WOULD NOT APPROVE OF.
A FEDORA THAT SELF-DESTRUCTS WHEN YOU TRY TO WEAR IT IN PUBLIC.

NEW MUSES

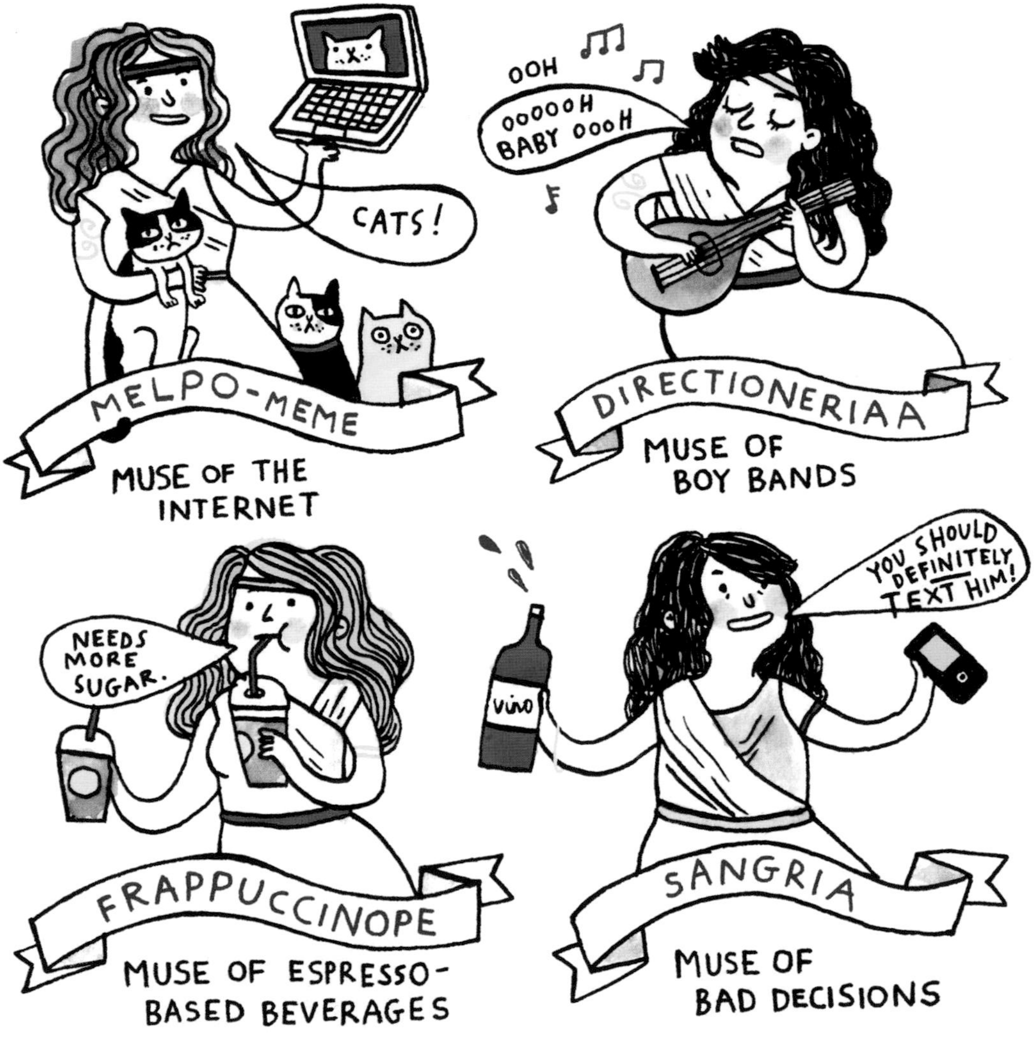
CATS!
MELPO-MEME
MUSE OF THE INTERNET
OOH
OOOOOH BABY OOOH
DIRECTIONERIAA
MUSE OF BOY BANDS
NEEDS MORE SUGAR.
FRAPPUCCINOPE
MUSE OF ESPRESSO-BASED BEVERAGES
VINO
YOU SHOULD DEFINITELY TEXT HIM!
SANGRIA
MUSE OF BAD DECISIONS

SNOW WHITE AND THE SEVEN TROLLS

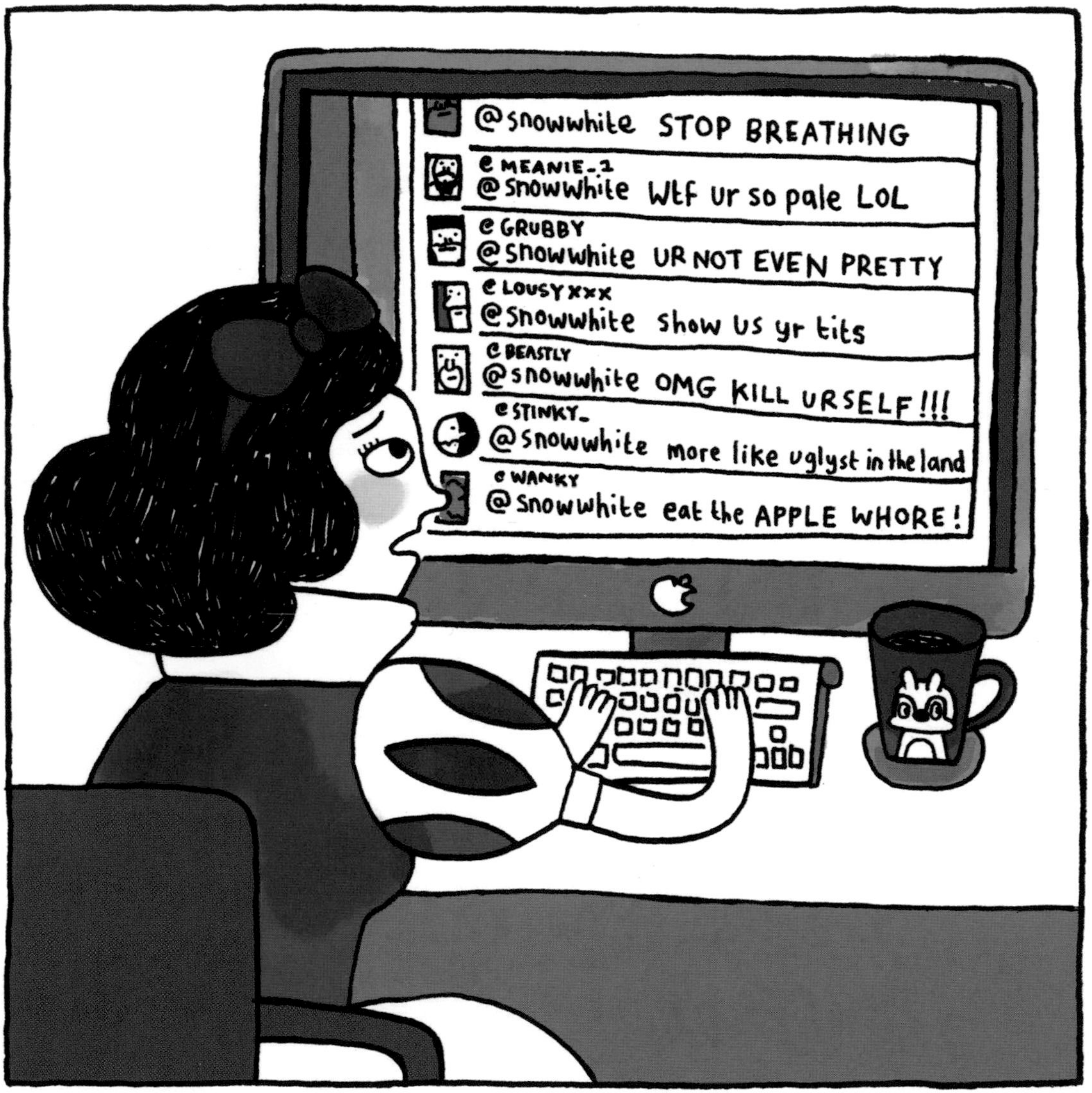
@snowwhite STOP BREATHING
@MEANIE_1
@snowwhite Wtf ur so pale LOL
@GRUBBY
@snowwhite UR NOT EVEN PRETTY
@LOUSYxxx
@snowwhite show us yr tits
@BEASTLY
@snowwhite OMG KILL URSELF!!!
@STINKY_
@snowwhite more like uglyst in the land
@WANKY
@snowwhite eat the APPLE WHORE!

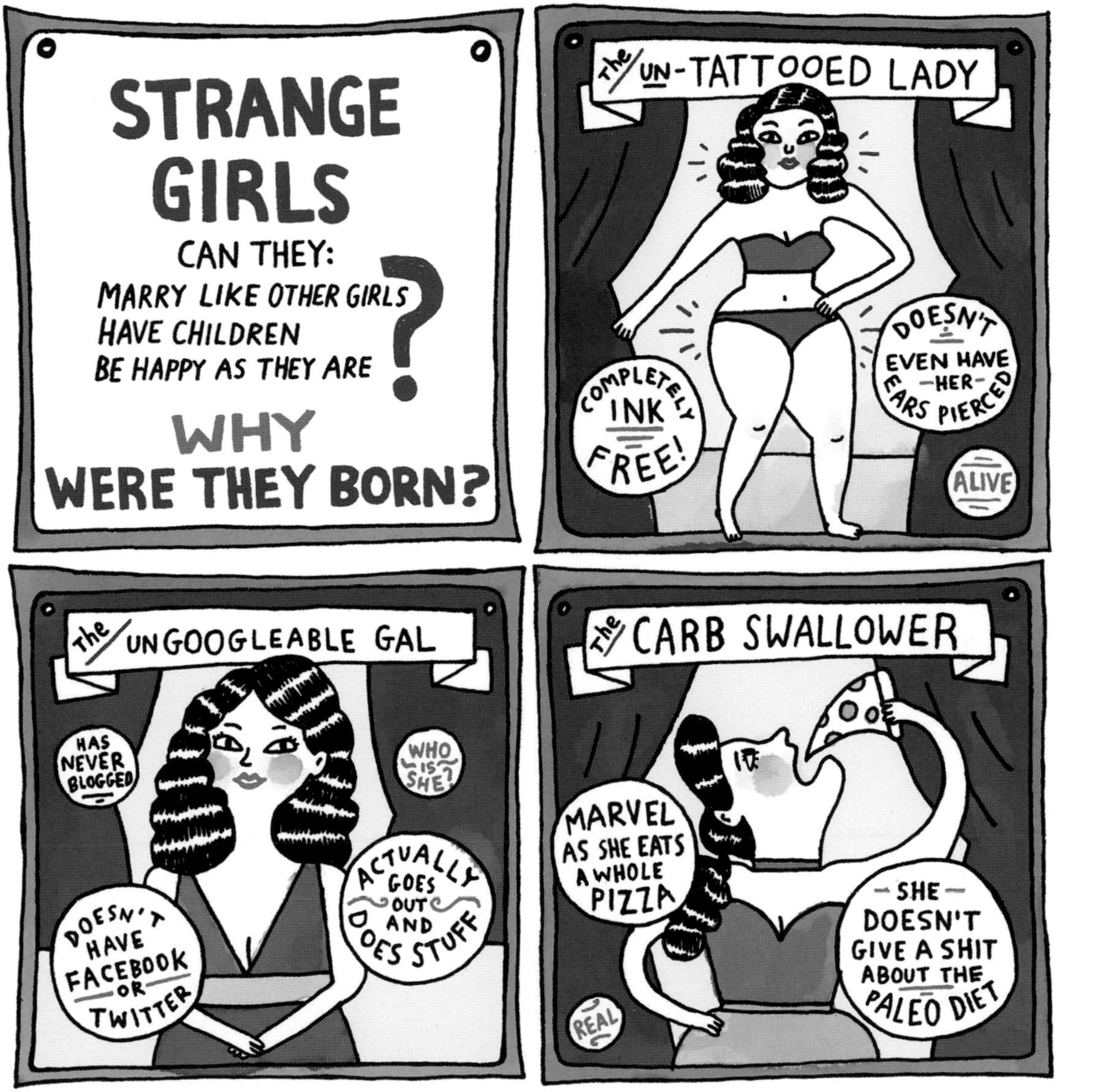
STRANGE GIRLS
CAN THEY:
MARRY LIKE OTHER GIRLS
HAVE CHILDREN
BE HAPPY AS THEY ARE
?
WHY
WERE THEY BORN?
The UN-TATTOOED LADY
COMPLETELY INK FREE!
DOESN'T EVEN HAVE HER EARS PIERCED
ALIVE
The UNGOOGLEABLE GAL
HAS NEVER BLOGGED
WHO IS SHE?
DOESN'T HAVE FACEBOOK OR TWITTER
ACTUALLY GOES OUT AND DOES STUFF
The CARB SWALLOWER
MARVEL AS SHE EATS A WHOLE PIZZA
SHE DOESN'T GIVE A SHIT ABOUT THE PALEO DIET
REAL

Gemma Correll is a young, quite small English person with bad eyesight. Thanks to the wonders of spectacle technology, however, she manages to hold down a full-time job as a freelance cartoonist slash writer slash illustrator and bumps into things only occasionally.

Gemma has illustrated various things for clients, including Hallmark, Hèrmes, and Emirates Airlines, and publishes her cartoon "Four Eyes" at GoComics.com. Gemma is also responsible for that "Pugs Not Drugs" T-shirt that you're sick of seeing everywhere. She is herself the proud owner of two pugs—Mr. Pickles and Bella—as well as an impressive collection of plastic snow globes.

Andrews McMeel Publishing, LLC
an Andrews McMeel Universal company
1130 Walnut Street, Kansas City, Missouri 64106

www.andrewsmcmeel.com

15 16 17 18 19 SDB 10 9 8 7 6 5 4 3 2 1

ISBN: 978-1-4494-6600-8

Library of Congress Control Number: 2014948752

Editor: Grace Suh
Art director and designer: Julie Barnes
Production editor: Erika Kuster
Production manager: Tamara Haus
Demand planner: Sue Eikos

ATTENTION: SCHOOLS AND BUSINESSES
Andrews McMeel books are available at quantity discounts with bulk purchase for educational, business, or sales promotional use. For information, please e-mail the Andrews McMeel Publishing Special Sales Department: specialsales@amuniversal.com.